My First
DICTIONARY

Susan Miller, Ed.D.

Ball   **A**irplane   **F**rog

Susan Miller, Ed.D., is professor emeritus of early childhood education at Kutztown University of Pennsylvania. She has written for more than 250 journals, magazines, and books, including *Scholastic's Early Childhood Today, Childhood Education, Early Childhood News,* and the weekend activities for *Parent & Child* magazine. Miller is a frequent presenter at conferences for the National Association for the Education of Young Children and the Association of Childhood Education International Study.

Illustrations by Ted Williams
Photography by Brian Warling Photography and Siede Preis Photography
© 2019 Shutterstock

Published by Sequoia Children's Publishing,
a division of Phoenix International Publications, Inc.

8501 West Higgins Road, Suite 790
Chicago, Illinois 60631

59 Gloucester Place
London W1U 8JJ

Sequoia Children's Publishing and associated logo are trademarks and/or
registered trademarks of Sequoia Publishing & Media, LLC.

Active Minds® is a registered trademark of PIP and is registered in the United States.

www.sequoiakidsbooks.com

10 9 8 7 6 5 4 3 2 1

ISBN 978-1-64269-065-1

Why This Dictionary Is Helpful for Children

My First Dictionary is written for young children showing an interest in how to use words and letters. It is also for children beginning to learn to read who want to sharpen their writing and spelling skills.

At first, children may want to use the illustrations or photos on each page to match the meanings to the words. As their reading skills emerge, they will enjoy using the dictionary to spell words and look up their meanings. *My First Dictionary* is designed for young children to use alone or with the assistance of an adult.

What Is a Dictionary?

A dictionary is a very special type of book. It doesn't tell a story like most of the books children may be used to reading. Instead, it is filled with all kinds of information about words that will help children to read, write, or tell stories of their own.

The words in this dictionary come from many places. Some words are used every day, while others may be seen or heard on television. There are words about groups of things that interest children (such as animals or toys) and words from vocabulary lists that teachers think children should know.

The words in a dictionary are arranged differently than in other books. The words are arranged in lists that go down the page, rather than across the page in sentences and paragraphs. A dictionary is easy to use when you understand how it is designed.

Using Definitions

The meaning of a word, or the *definition*, tells something about it. There are usually one or two sentences that give this information. Some words have more than one meaning and can be used in different ways. The various meanings a word has are given separately and have numbers in front of them.

Often, readers will see a sentence written in *italics* after the definition. That lets them see how they can use the word. Frequently, a picture or photo will give another clue about how the word is used.

The Way Words Are Used

Sometimes words can have different spellings depending on how they are used. For instance, *rests* and *resting* are forms of the word *rest*, but they are spelled differently because they have slightly different uses. Words that describe more than one thing are called plural. Most words simply add an s to become plural (*doll, dolls*), but others change in special ways. The word mouse, for example, changes to mice when there is more than one mouse. Other words add an es (*glass, glasses*). In a few words, the final y changes to i, and an es is added (*story, stories*). In *My First Dictionary*, you can see how a word becomes plural. Right below the entry word, you will sometimes see plurals in parentheses ( ). Words that add s to become plural will not appear in parentheses, but words that become plural in any other way will feature their plural form in the parentheses.

Other words describe action. They can also change their spelling depending on how they are used. When someone is speaking about something that happened in the past or the present, the spelling will sometimes change. Examples of this are *look, looks, looked, looking* and *go, goes,* *went, gone, going*. In *My First Dictionary*, every action word will be followed by parentheses that include how the word is used for something that happens now, for something that happened in the past, and for something that is in the middle of happening now. As an example, the word drink will be followed by (*drinks, drank, drinking*).

Some words that compare things change their spelling, as well. Many times these words add er for more and est for the most (such as *fast, faster, fastest*). Other words change their spelling completely (such as *good, better, best*). Words in parentheses will demonstrate how these words are spelled when they refer to more and most.

Finally, readers will notice that most words begin with lowercase letters. However, some words begin with uppercase, capital letters. Words for holidays, such as *Thanksgiving*, days, such as *Monday*, and months, such as *November*, start with capital letters.

All Set to Begin

My First Dictionary will be an exciting tool to help children use and find out more about words as they read, write, spell, and listen to others. Remember that children learn best with the help of adults such as parents and teachers, so children should always be ready to ask for help if they need it.

a

A means one of something. *They rode to school on **a** bus.*

about

1. **About** means almost. *Four cookies are **about** a handful.* 2. Sometimes **about** means nearby. *The children are playing **about**.*

above

Above means higher than something. *The pear is **above** the lemon.*

acorn

An **acorn** is a kind of nut that grows on an oak tree. *Squirrels like to eat **acorns**.*

across

If you go **across** something, you go from one side to the other. *The boy walked **across** the road.*

act

(acts, acted, acting)
When people take part in a play, they **act** in it. *The boys were **acting** like knights in the play.*

add

(adds, added, adding)
If you **add** things, you put them together. *You **add** one block on top of another to build a tower.*

address

(addresses)
An **address** tells people where you live. *You write an **address** on a letter before you mail it.*

adult

An **adult** is a grown-up person such as your teacher.

afraid

If you are **afraid**, you think something is bad or scary.

afternoon

The **afternoon** is the part of the day that happens after the morning.

again

Again means something occurs once more. *The child asked to sing the favorite song **again**.*

age

Your **age** tells how old you are. Your **age** is the number of years you have been alive.

ahead

When you are **ahead**, you are in front of something. *You win the race when you finish ahead of the other runners.*

air

Air is a gas we breathe. *The air is all around us.*

airplane

An **airplane** is a machine that flies through the air. People can sit inside an **airplane** when they fly. An **airplane** has wings and an engine.

album

An **album** is a book that holds pictures. *You can put pictures of your family in a photo album.*

alike

If two things are **alike**, they are the same in some way. *An orange and an apple are alike because they are both fruit.*

all

All means every one. *All of the cookies are round.*

alligator

An **alligator** is a scaly animal with a long mouth, sharp teeth, and a long tail. An **alligator** can swim in water or walk on land.

almond

An **almond** is a kind of nut with a light brown shell. Some candy bars contain **almonds**.

alone

When you are **alone**, you are not with other people.

alphabet

The **alphabet** has all the letters that make words. There are 26 letters from *A to Z* in the **alphabet**.

also

Also means in addition to. *You may also get some pizza to go with your juice.*

am

(be, are, is, was, were, been, being)
Am means that someone or something exists. *I am the best bike rider.*

among

Among means in between or in the middle of things. *The pear is **among** the lemons.*

an

An means one of something. *You are eating **an** apple.*

and

And is used to connect two things. *You need a ball **and** a bat to play baseball.*

angry

(angrier, angriest)
If you are **angry**, you feel mad and upset. *An **angry** person may want to yell.*

animal

An **animal** lives, moves, and breathes. *People, dogs, birds, and fish are **animals**.*

answer

(answers, answered, answering)
1. When you **answer**, you talk to someone who asked you a question.
2. What you say or write down after a question is an **answer**.

ant

An **ant** is a tiny crawling insect. Most **ants** live in tunnels underground.

any

1. **Any** means one is not more important than another. If you can chose **any**, it doesn't matter which one you choose. *You may pick **any** flower.* 2. **Any** also means an uncertain amount. *Is there **any** ice cream left?*

anything

1. **Anything** means one item is not more important than another. *You may play with **anything** in the toy box.*
2. **Anything** also means an uncertain thing. *Is there **anything** to do?*

ape

An **ape** is a hairy animal that can stand up straight. An **ape** is like a big monkey without a tail.

apple

An **apple** is a fruit that grows on trees. An **apple** is juicy and crunchy with red, green, or yellow skin.

April

April is the fourth month of the year. **April** is in the springtime.

are

(am, be, is, was, were, been, being) **Are** means something occurs or lives. *You are going to school on the bus.*

arm

Your **arm** connects your shoulder and hand.

arm

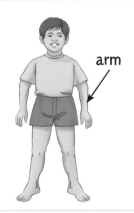

art

Something that someone has made, like a painting or drawing, is **art**.

artist

An **artist** is a person who draws, paints, or makes music.

as

As means like. *You are pretty as a picture.*

astronaut

An **astronaut** is a person who goes into space. An **astronaut** wears a special suit and helmet.

at

At indicates a point in time or a place. *We will meet at one o'clock at the park.*

athlete

An **athlete** is a person who plays sports. **Athletes** can run, jump, and move around very well.

August

August is the eighth month of the year. **August** occurs in the summer.

aunt

Your **aunt** is the sister of your father or mother, or the wife of your uncle.

avocado

An **avocado** is a green or purple fruit that grows on trees. When ripe, an **avocado** is soft inside.

A B C D E F G H I J K L M N O P Q R S T U V W X Y Z

baby
(babies)
A **baby** is a very young child.

bad
(worse, worst)
1. If someone misbehaves, he is being naughty or **bad**. 2. If food is too old or not good to eat, it is **bad**.

badge
A person wears a **badge** to tell who she is. A **badge** may have the person's name or let you know about her job, like being a police officer.

bag
A **bag** is used to hold and carry things. **Bags** are made of paper, cloth, plastic, or leather.

bagel
A **bagel** is a chewy kind of bread shaped like a donut.

bake
(bakes, baked, baking)
You cook foods, such as bread or cookies, when you **bake** them in the oven. *We baked a birthday cake.*

baker
A **baker** is someone who cooks things in the oven. A **baker** sells the cakes and pies he baked.

ball
1. A **ball** is a round toy you roll, bounce, hit, throw, or catch. 2. A **ball** is a party where lots of people dance.

ballet
Ballet is a type of dancing where people spin and leap.

balloon
A **balloon** is a thin rubber or plastic bag that gets bigger when filled with air. Some balloons can float in the air.

banana
A **banana** is a long, curved fruit. A **banana** has yellow skin and a soft, white, tasty inside.

band

1. A **band** is a group of people who play music together. 2. A **band** is a thin piece of material that goes around something.

barn

A **barn** is a big building on a farm where the farmer keeps animals, hay, and machines.

baseball

1. A **baseball** is a hard ball the size of an apple.
2. **Baseball** is a game played by two teams with a ball and bat.

basketball

1. A **basketball** is a big ball that bounces.
2. In the game **basketball**, two teams try to throw the ball through a hoop.

bat

1. A **bat** is a stick used to hit a ball. 2. A **bat** is a small animal with wings that flies at night and sometimes lives in a cave.

be

(am, are, is, was, were, been, being)
Be is used to show something occurs or something exists. *You can **be** a good baseball player if you practice.*

beach

(beaches)

A **beach** is a sandy place by the sea or a lake. You can swim and play at the **beach**.

bean

A **bean** is a kind of seed inside a vegetable. People eat many kinds of **beans** —kidney, lima, coffee, and green beans.

bear

A **bear** is a large furry animal. Many **bears** sleep all winter.

beard

A **beard** is the hair that grows on a man's chin and cheeks.

beautiful

If something is **beautiful**, it is lovely to see, to hear, or to smell.

because

Because tells the reason for something. *You are going to the store **because** you have run out of milk.*

bed

A **bed** is a soft place to lie down and rest or sleep.

bee

A **bee** is a small, flying, black-and-yellow insect that makes honey. If a **bee** gets angry, it might sting you.

beetle

A **beetle** is a tiny insect with six legs. A **beetle** has hard wings.

before

1. **Before** means at an earlier time. *You got to school **before** I did.* 2. **Before** means in front of somebody or something. *The number one comes **before** two when you are counting.*

begin

(begins, began, begun, beginning)
If you **begin** something, you start it.

behind

If something is **behind** something else, it is at the back of it. *The pear is **behind** the lemon.*

bell

If you hit a **bell**, it makes a ringing sound. **Bells** are hollow and usually made of metal.

below

If something is **below** another thing, it is under it. *The pear is **below** the lemon.*

bench

(benches)
A **bench** is a type of seat long enough for several people to sit on.

berry

(berries)
A **berry** is a small, soft fruit with lots of seeds. There are many kinds of **berries**, such as blueberries, raspberries, and strawberries.

better

(good, best)
1. If you are feeling **better**, you are not as sick as you had been. 2. If you are good at something and practice hard, you will become **better** at it.

between

If something is **between** two things, it is in the middle of them. *The pear is **between** the lemons.*

bicycle

A **bicycle** is a machine you can ride. A **bicycle** has two wheels and a handlebar. You sit on the seat of the **bicycle** and pedal with your feet to make it go.

big

(bigger, biggest)
Big means something is not small.

bird

A **bird** is an animal with a beak, wings, and feathers. Most **birds** can fly.

black

Black is the darkest color of all.

blanket

A **blanket** is a warm, thick cover for a bed.

block

(blocks, blocked, blocking)
1. If something **blocks** your way, you can't get through.
2. A **block** is a toy made out of wood or plastic that you can build with.

blood

Blood is a liquid that flows through veins inside your body.

blow

(blows, blew, blown, blowing)
When you **blow** air out of your mouth, or the wind **blows**, air moves.

blue

On a clear day, the sky is the color **blue**.

blueberry

(blueberries)
A **blueberry** is a small, round, soft juicy fruit. **Blueberries** grow in bunches on a bush.

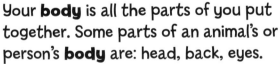

boat

A **boat** floats on the water and carries people or things. **Boats** move by engines, sails, or paddles.

body

(bodies)
Your **body** is all the parts of you put together. Some parts of an animal's or person's **body** are: head, back, eyes.

bone

A **bone** is the hard part inside your body under your skin. All of your **bones** together are called a skeleton.

book

A **book** is made up of a cover with sheets of paper inside called pages. You can look at pictures and read the words in a **book**.

boot

A **boot** is a tall shoe that covers your foot and part of your leg. **Boots** keep your feet warm and dry in cold, wet weather.

born

When a baby is **born**, its life begins outside of its mother.

both

Both means one and the other. *You and your sister are **both** playing with dolls.*

bottle

A **bottle** holds liquids. People can sometimes drink the liquid in a **bottle**, but sometimes they cannot. A baby's **bottle** has a special cap called a nipple.

bottom

The **bottom** of something, such as a lamp, is the base or the lowest part.

bowl

(bowls, bowled, bowling)
1. When you **bowl**, you play a game to knock down pins with a bowling ball. 2. A **bowl** is a deep, round dish that holds food.

boy

A **boy** is a male child who grows up to be a man.

bread

Bread is a food made from flour and water and then baked in an oven. You can cut **bread** into slices to eat in a sandwich.

breakfast

Breakfast is the first meal of the day. When you eat **breakfast**, you might have bread, fruit, and juice.

breathe

(breathes, breathed, breathing)
When you **breathe**, you bring air into your body through your nose and mouth and then send it out again.

brick

A **brick** is a block of baked clay. Many **bricks** stacked together make walls and buildings.

bright

(brighter, brightest)
1. A **bright** color or light is strong and easy to see. 2. If someone is very smart, she is **bright**.

bring

(brings, brought, bringing)
If you **bring** something, you carry it with you.

broccoli

You eat the green stalk and buds of the green vegetable, **broccoli**.

brother

Your **brother** is a boy who has the same mother or father as you.

brown

Brown is a dark color, like that of chocolate or toast.

bubble

A **bubble** is a thin skin of soap with a ball of air inside.

bug

A **bug** is any kind of small insect. A **bug** can move by flying, crawling, or jumping.

build

(builds, built, building)
If you **build** something, you put all of the parts together.

building

A **building** is a place that people create with walls and a roof. People live and work in **buildings** such as houses, schools, or barns.

bull

A **bull** is a male cow, a large farm animal with two long horns on its head. The **bull** eats grass and does not give milk.

bully

(bullies)
A **bully** is someone who is mean and hurts or frightens others.

bunny

(bunnies)
A **bunny** is a soft furry rabbit with long ears. A **bunny** uses its back legs to hop.

bus

(buses)
A **bus** is a big vehicle that carries a lot of people from place to place. A **bus** has lots of seats and windows but just one driver.

butter

Butter is a light-yellow food made from cream from a cow. You can cook with it or spread soft **butter** on toast.

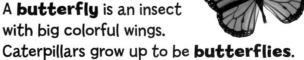

butterfly

(butterflies)
A **butterfly** is an insect with big colorful wings. Caterpillars grow up to be **butterflies**.

cabbage

A **cabbage** is a vegetable that grows into a head of leaves.

cactus

(cacti)

A **cactus** is a thorny plant that grows in the desert. A **cactus** needs very little water to live.

cake

A **cake** is made by baking a mixture of flour, sugar, eggs, and milk in the oven. You put candles on a birthday **cake**.

calculator

People do number problems on a machine called a **calculator**.

calendar

A **calendar** shows the days, weeks, and months of the year. People mark important dates on a **calendar**.

call

(calls, called, calling)

1. If you **call** someone, you can talk to them on the phone. 2. When you **call** out to someone, you speak loudly and want them to come over to you.

camera

You can take photographs with a **camera**.

camp

(camps, camped, camping)

When you **camp**, you live in a tent outdoors for a short time.

can

1. **Can** means you are able to do something. *They can jump very high.* 2. A **can** is made of metal and opens on one end. A **can** holds foods and drinks, such as soda.

candy

(candies)

Candy is a tasty sweet food made with sugar. Some **candy** is soft, while other **candy** is hard and crunchy.

cap

1. A **cap** is a soft hat with a round part at the front to shade your eyes. 2. A **cap** is a small lid, like the one on toothpaste.

car

A **car** is a machine with an engine and four wheels that people ride in. You drive a **car** on a road.

carrot

A **carrot** is a long, crunchy orange vegetable that grows underground.

cash

Cash is money. **Cash** can be coins or paper bills. You use **cash** to buy things.

castle

A **castle** is a big, strong stone building with thick walls and towers. Long ago, a **castle** kept the king, queen, and other people who lived inside safe from attackers.

cat

A **cat** is a furry animal with a tail. Small **cats** live in peoples' houses as pets. Large **cats**, like lions and tigers, live in the wild.

catch

(catches, caught, catching)
1. When you get a hold of something that's moving, like a ball, you **catch** it.
2. If you **catch** an illness, you become sick.

caterpillar

A **caterpillar** is small and long, like a worm, with little legs. A **caterpillar** changes into a moth or butterfly.

cave

A **cave** is a large hole in the side of a mountain or under the ground.

celery

People eat the crunchy stem of **celery**, a green vegetable.

cent

A **cent** is a very small amount of money. A penny is worth one **cent**, a quarter is worth 25 **cents**, and a dollar is worth 100 **cents**.

cereal

Cereal is a breakfast food usually made out of corn, wheat, or oats and served with milk.

chair

A **chair** is a seat with a back for one person to sit on.

chalk

Chalk, made from a soft rock, comes in white and colored sticks. You can draw or write with **chalk** on a chalkboard.

A B C D E F G H I J K L M N O P Q R S T U V W X Y Z

checkers

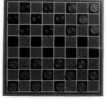

In the game of **checkers**, you move flat, round, red or black pieces around a checkered board.

cheese

Cheese is a yellow or white food made from milk. You might eat **cheese** on pizza or in a sandwich.

chess

Chess is a board game for two players. To win at **chess**, you must capture the other player's king.

chest

1. A **chest** is a big heavy box with a lid to store special things inside.
2. Your **chest** is the front part of your body below your neck and between your arms.

chick

A **chick** is a young chicken or other bird. A **chick** makes a *peep-peep* sound.

chicken

A **chicken** is a bird that farmers raise for eggs and meat to eat.

child

(children)

A **child** is a young boy or girl. When **children** grow up they become men and women.

chimpanzee

A **chimpanzee** is a hairy type of ape that is smaller than a gorilla.

chin

Your **chin** is the part of your face that is below your mouth.

chocolate

Chocolate is a sweet brown food used in candy, cakes, and drinks. **Chocolate** comes from the brown beans of the cocoa tree.

Christmas

Christmas is a holiday on December 25 to celebrate the birth of Christ. People give gifts to each other on **Christmas**.

circle

A **circle** is a round shape like a ring.

circus

(circuses)

A **circus** is a group of people, such as clowns and acrobats, and animals, such as elephants and tigers, that travels around and performs shows.

city
(cities)

A **city** is a very big town where many people work and live.

clay

Clay is soft earth. People make things from **clay**, like bricks, pots, and cups.

clean
(cleans, cleaned, cleaning)

When you **clean** something, you get rid of the dirt.

climb
(climbs, climbed, climbing)

If you **climb**, you move up something tall, like a ladder, using your hands and feet to hold on.

clock

A **clock** is a machine with numbers that tells the time. The short hand on the **clock** tells the hour, and the long hand tells the minutes.

clothes

Clothes are the things you wear, like pants or a shirt. **Clothes**, like a coat, cover your skin and keep you warm.

cloud

A **cloud** is a white or gray shape that floats in the sky. **Clouds** are made of many tiny drops of water. Rain falls from dark clouds.

clown

A **clown** is a person who dresses up funny and does silly things to make you laugh. Sometimes you see a **clown** at the circus.

coach
(coaches)

A **coach** is a person who trains and manages players on a sports team, such as baseball.

coat

A **coat** is an article of clothing you wear over your other clothes to keep warm when you go outdoors.

cocoa

Chocolate comes from the brown beans of the **cocoa** tree. People like to drink sweetened hot **cocoa**.

coconut

A **coconut** is a large, brown, round, hard-shelled nut that grows on the **coconut** tree. People eat the chewy white fruit inside a **coconut**.

coffee

Coffee is a brown drink made by adding water to the roasted beans of the **coffee** plant.

coin

A **coin** is a small, round piece of money made from metal. Pennies, nickels, dimes, and quarters are **coins**.

cold

(colder, coldest)

1. If you have a **cold**, you are sick and sneeze or cough a lot. 2. Snow and ice feel **cold** because they are not hot.

color

Color is a way to describe how something looks. *A rainbow has many different* **colors**, *like red, orange, and yellow.*

come

(comes, came, coming)

1. When you **come**, you move forward toward something. 2. If you want to know when the train will arrive, you ask when it will **come**.

compass

(compasses)

So you won't get lost, a **compass** has a needle that shows direction by pointing north.

cook

(cooks, cooked, cooking)

When you **cook**, you make or heat food so it is ready to eat. 2. A **cook** is a person who makes or heats food to eat.

cookie

A **cookie** is a small, sweet cake that is baked in the oven. **Cookies** are flat and can be crispy or chewy.

cool

(cooler, coolest)

If something feels **cool**, it is a bit cold.

corn

Farmers grow **corn**, a plant with tall stalks and yellow seed kernels inside ears. You eat **corn** on the cob, and you can pop seeds of **corn** to make popcorn.

costume

A **costume** is a special set of clothes that an actor or a child wears to pretend to be someone else.

couch

(couches)

A **couch** is a long piece of furniture that is soft to sit on.

cover
(covers, covered, covering)
1. If you **cover** a thing, you put something over it to keep it warm. *Cover the horse with a blanket so it won't be cold.* 2. A **cover** can hide something. *Put a cover over the baby to play peek-a-boo.*

cow
A **cow** is a large farm animal that eats grass and moos. Some **cows** give milk.

cowboy
A **cowboy** or cowgirl lives on a ranch, rides a horse, and takes care of cows.

crab
A **crab** is an ocean animal with a hard shell and sharp pinching claws.

crawl
(crawls, crawled, crawling)
When you **crawl**, you move along on your hands and knees.

crayon
A **crayon** is a waxy type of colored pencil for drawing.

crib
A **crib** is a bed with tall sides so a baby won't fall out.

crocodile
A **crocodile** is a large animal with a long tail and big sharp teeth. A **crocodile** lives in rivers and swamps in some hot places.

cry
(cries, cried, crying)
You **cry** if you are sad or hurt and tears fall from your eyes.

cub
A **cub** is a baby animal. Baby bears, foxes, wolves, lions, and tigers are cubs.

cup
A **cup** is a container for drinks. A **cup** has a handle.

cupcake
A **cupcake** is a small tasty cake you bake in the oven. Some **cupcakes** are spread with sweet icing.

curtain
A **curtain** is a long piece of fabric that covers a window.

D

daisy
(daisies)
A **daisy** is a flower with a yellow center and white petals.

dance
(dances, danced, dancing)
When you **dance**, you move your body and feet in time with music.

dandelion
A bright yellow flower, the **dandelion** grows in fields and on lawns.

danger
When there is **danger**, something bad could happen to you.

dark
(darker, darkest) **Dark** means something isn't light. The night is **dark**.

daughter
Somebody's **daughter** is a girl who is that person's child.

day
1. **Day** is a time when it is light outside. 2. A **day** is 24 hours long—from one midnight to the next.

dead
If a plant or animal is **dead**, it is not living anymore.

December
December is the last month of the year. **December** is in the winter.

deer
(deer)
A **deer** is a big forest animal with short brown fur and long legs for running fast. The male **deer** has big horns on its head called antlers.

desk
A **desk** is a type of table with drawers where you can write or use your computer.

dessert
A **dessert** is a sweet treat, like cake or fruit, that you eat at the end of a meal.

A B C D E F G H I J K L M N O P Q R S T U V W X Y Z

diary
(diaries)

A **diary** is a blank book in which you write about what is happening to you.

dig
(digs, dug, digging)

If you **dig**, you make a hole in the ground by removing the dirt.

dime

A **dime** is a small, shiny, round metal coin. A **dime** is worth ten cents.

dinner

Dinner is the biggest meal of the day. Many people eat their **dinner** at night.

dinosaur

A **dinosaur** is an animal that lived a long, long time ago. Some **dinosaurs**, such as *Tyrannosaurus rex*, were giants.

dirt

Dirt is mud or soil that makes something unclean.

dish
(dishes)

A **dish** is something you put food on or in when you eat. Plates and bowls are types of **dishes**.

dive
(dives, dived, diving)

When you **dive** into the water, you jump in with your arms and head first.

do
(does, did, done, doing)

When you **do** something, you make something or you make something happen. *When you draw a card for Mommy, you **do** it all by yourself.*

doctor

A **doctor** is someone who helps sick people get better.

dog

A **dog** is a furry animal that barks. Some **dogs** live in a house as a pet, while others do work, like guarding buildings or farm animals.

doll

A **doll** is a small toy that can look like a child or an adult.

dollar

A kind of money, a **dollar** looks like a piece of green paper. One **dollar** is worth 100 cents, the same as 100 pennies or 4 quarters.

A B C D E F G H I J K L M N O P Q R S T U V W X Y Z

dolphin

A **dolphin** is a big, smart animal that lives in the ocean. A **dolphin** is not a fish. A **dolphin** blows air through a hole on its head.

door

You open a **door** when you need to go into a room or building, and you close the **door** behind you when you leave.

doughnut

A **doughnut** is a round, sweet cake with a hole in the middle.

down

Down is the direction something takes to move from a higher place to a lower one. *The ball rolls **down** the hill.*

dozen

A **dozen** is a group of 12 things, like a **dozen** eggs in a box.

dragon

A **dragon** is a huge make-believe monster with scales, wings, a long tail, and fiery breath. **Dragons** appear in many stories.

draw

(draws, drew, drawing)
When you **draw**, you make a picture with a pencil, a pen, or crayons.

drawing

A **drawing** is a picture you make with a pencil, a pen, or crayons.

dream

(dreams, dreamed, dreaming)
When you **dream**, pictures and thoughts go through your mind after you are asleep.

dress

(dresses, dressed, dressing)
1. When you **dress**, you put your clothes on. 2. A **dress** is a skirt and top sewn together for girls to wear.

drink

(drinks, drank, drinking)
1. When you pour a liquid, like juice, into your mouth and swallow it, you are **drinking**. 2. A **drink** is a liquid, such as water, that you swallow when you are thirsty.

drum

A **drum** is a round, hollow musical instrument that you can tap with sticks or your hands.

dry

(dries, dried, drying, drier, driest)
1. When you **dry** something, like rubbing it with a towel, you take the water off of it.
2. Something that is **dry** is not wet.

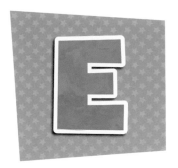

E

each

Each means every thing or every person. *The father gave **each** one of his children a cupcake for a snack.*

eagle

An **eagle** is a large bird with a sharp curved beak and long wings. An **eagle** catches other birds.

ear

An **ear** is the part of your body that you use to hear. You have one **ear** on each side of your head.

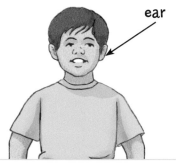

ear

early

(earlier, earliest)
Early means before something starts. If you arrive **early**, you get somewhere sooner than you expected.

Earth

1. We live on the planet **Earth**, which includes all of the oceans and land.
2. You can plant things in the **earth**, or ground.

east

The direction in which the sun comes up in the morning is **east**.

Easter

Easter is a special Christian holiday that occurs in the spring. *Children enjoy hunting for colored **Easter** eggs during the **Easter** holiday.*

easy

(easier, easiest)
If something is **easy**, it is not very hard for someone to do.

eat

(eats, ate, eaten, eating)
When you **eat**, you place food in your mouth, chew it, and then swallow it.

edge

The **edge** is the part along the side or end of something. *The doll sits on the **edge** of the chair.*

A B C D E F G H I J K L M N O P Q R S T U V W X Y Z

egg

An **egg** is a smooth round object that may have a baby bird, fish, reptile, or insect growing inside of it. Chickens lay **eggs** with a hard shell. Some people cook and eat **eggs.**

eight

Eight is a number that is one more than seven.

eighteen

Eighteen is a number that is one more than seventeen. 17+1=18.

eighty

Eighty is a number that is eight groups of 10. 8x10=80.

elephant

An **elephant** is the largest land animal. An **elephant** is gray with a long nose called a trunk and two huge ears.

eleven

Eleven is a number that is one more than ten.

empty

(emptier, emptiest)
When something is **empty**, it has nothing inside.

end

The last part of something is the **end.** *You are finished listening to the CD now that you are at the **end**.*

English

English is the main language spoken in the United States, Canada, England, and some other countries.

enough

If you have **enough** of something, you have as much as you need. *When you eat until you are full, you have had **enough** to eat.*

enter

(enters, entered, entering)
You go into a place when you **enter** it.

envelope

An **envelope** is a folded paper cover for a letter that you glue shut. On the front of an **envelope**, you place a stamp and write the address.

erase

(erases, erased, erasing)
When you **erase** something, you wipe it out so it can no longer be seen.

eraser

When you rub with an **eraser**, it wipes away pencil marks from paper. Some pencils have a small **eraser** on the end.

escape

(escapes, escaped, escaping)
When you **escape**, you get away from something.

even

1. An **even** number is one that you can divide by two. The opposite of an **even** number (2, 4...) is an odd number (3, 5...).
2. If something is flat or level, like a floor, it is **even**.

evening

Evening is the part of day between afternoon and night. The sun goes down in the **evening**.

ever

1. **Ever** means for all time. *At the end of the story, the man and woman lived happily **ever** after.* 2. **Ever** means at any time at all. *Have you **ever** played soccer?*

every

Every means each of a group without exception. *You must pick up **every** toy from the floor.*

except

Except means someone or something is left out. *Everyone **except** the baby, who is too young, went to the movies.*

exercise

(exercises, exercised, exercising)

1. When you **exercise**, you do an activity to develop or improve your body. We **exercise** our legs by running.
2. An **exercise** is a small bit of work you do to help you learn something. You can practice an **exercise** on your piano.

extra

Extra means more of something than usual. *Would you like to eat an **extra** scoop of ice cream?*

eye

Your **eye** is the part of your face you use to see.

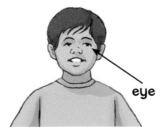

eye

A B C D E F G H I J K L M N O P Q R S T U V W X Y Z

face

Your **face** is the front part of your head. Your eyes, nose, and mouth are on your **face**.

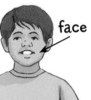
face

falcon

A **falcon** is a bird with powerful wings, good eyes, and a pointed beak. A **falcon** is a good hunter.

fall

(falls, fell, fallen, falling)
1. If something **falls**, it suddenly goes down toward the ground. 2. **Fall** is the season of the year between summer and winter.

family

(families)
A **family** is a group of related people, such as children, parents, and grandparents.

fan

1. A **fan** is an object that moves or blows air around to make you feel cool. 2. A **fan** is a person who admires someone else's skills. *The fans cheer when the player catches the baseball.*

far

(farther, farthest)
Far means a long way. *The moon is far away from Earth.*

farm

A **farm** is a piece of land where a farmer grows food and raises animals.

farmer

A **farmer** is a person who works on a farm taking care of the animals and the crops.

fast

(faster, fastest)
If someone or something moves along quickly, that person or thing goes **fast**.

fat

(fatter, fattest)
A **fat** animal or person has a big, round body.

father

A **father** is a man who has a child.

February

February is a winter month and the second month of the year. *Valentine's Day is in February.*

feed

(feeds, fed, feeding)
When you **feed** someone or something, you give that person or thing food to eat.

feet

1. You have two **feet** on the end of your legs. You stand on your **feet**. 2. Feet are a measurement. There are three **feet** in one yard.

feet

fence

A **fence** is a kind of outside wall made of wood or metal. A **fence** around a farm keeps the animals in.

fifteen

Fifteen is a number that is one more than fourteen. 10+5=15.

fifty

Fifty is a number that means five groups of ten. 10+10+10+10+10=50.

find

(finds, found, finding)
When you **find** something, you see something that was lost. *The baby finds his toy under the chair.*

finger

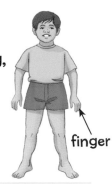

Your **fingers** are the five long, thin parts at the end of your hand. Your **fingers** bend so you can pick up things. Your thumb is one of your **fingers**.

finger

fire

Fire is the hot, bright light that happens when something burns. A **fire** keeps you warm.

firefighter

A **firefighter** is a person who puts out a fire with water from a hose. **Firefighters** wear heavy boots and helmets so they don't get burned.

fire truck

Firefighters ride to put out a fire on a **fire truck**. **Fire trucks** carry hoses and ladders.

first

1. **First** means at the front or at the beginning. When you win a race, you come in **first**. 2. **First** is number one in a series you count.

fish

(fishes, fished, fishing)
1. When you **fish**, you use a net or fishing pole to catch the **fish**. 2. A **fish** is an animal with scales that lives under water. A **fish** uses its fins and tail to swim.

five

Five is a number that is one more than four.

fix

(fixes, fixed, fixing)
When you **fix** something, you repair it or put it back together again.

flag

A **flag** is a piece of cloth you hang up with colored shapes or letters on it. Every country has its own **flag**.

flashlight

A **flashlight** is a small lamp you can hold in your hand to light up dark places.

flower

The **flower** is the part of a plant that has colored petals and smells good.

flute

A **flute** is a musical instrument that works like a whistle. You blow air into the **flute** and use the keys and finger holes to change sounds.

fly

(flies, flew, flown, flying)
1. When something **flies**, it moves through the air. A bird **flies** from tree to tree.
2. A **fly** is a small insect with wings that makes a buzzing sound.

fold

(folds, folded, folding)
When you **fold** something, you bend parts over each other. *After you **fold** the shirts, you put them in the basket.*

food

Food is all of the things that plants, animals, and people eat to stay healthy.

foot

(feet)
1. Your **foot** is the part of your body at the end of your leg. You stand on your **feet**.
2. A **foot** is a measurement. Twelve inches equals a **foot** on a ruler.

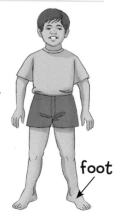

foot

football

1. A **football** is a ball that is round in the middle and pointed at the ends. 2. When you play the game of **football**, two teams throw, catch, and kick a **football** to score points.

for

For is used to show how something is used or where something goes. *A crayon is **for** drawing. The baker made the birthday cake **for** you.*

forest

A **forest** is a place where many trees grow together.

fork

A **fork** is a tool with a handle and several sharp points at the end. You use a **fork** to pick up food and eat.

forty

Forty is a number that is four groups of ten. 10+10+10+10=40.

four

Four is a number that is one more than three. *A horse has **four** legs.*

fourteen

Fourteen is a number that is one less than fifteen.

fox
(foxes)

A **fox** is a wild, furry animal that has pointy ears and a long, bushy tail. A **fox** is smaller than most dogs.

frame

A **frame** is a border around a picture.

free
(freer, freest)

1. If something is **free**, there is no charge and you do not pay for it. 2. When something is **free** or loose, it can go anywhere.

Friday

Friday is the day of the week that comes after Thursday.

friend

A **friend** is a person who you know very well and like a great deal.

frog

A **frog** is a small animal that leaps on land and swims in the water with its strong back legs. **Frogs** eat flies.

front

The part that comes first or you see first is the **front**. *The **front** of a book is-the cover.*

frown
(frowns, frowned, frowning)

When you **frown**, your face wrinkles to show you are mad or sad.

fruit

The **fruit** is the part of the plant that has seeds in it. We like to eat **fruits**, such as apples and blueberries.

fun

When you are having **fun**, you are having a good time and enjoying yourself.

game

A **game** is something with rules that you play for fun.
Basketball and chess are games.

garbage

Garbage is all the things you throw away. People put **garbage** in large bags or cans, but it may still get smelly.

garden

A **garden** is a piece of land near your home where you grow flowers and vegetables.

gas

(gases)

People go to the gas station to put **gas** in their cars and trucks. Liquid **gas** burns inside the car's engine to make it go.

gate

A **gate** is like a door in a fence or a wall. *When the gate is open, you can drive the tractor to the barn.*

get

(gets, got, gotten, getting)

When you **get** something, you obtain it. *If you are hungry, you need to get some breakfast.*

gift

A **gift** is something special that you give to someone. You might wrap a **gift** with colored paper and a bow.

giraffe

A **giraffe** is a wild African animal with a very long neck, long legs, and brown spots. **Giraffes** eat leaves from tall trees.

girl

A **girl** is a female child who will grow up to be a woman.

give

(gives, gave, given, giving)

If you **give** another person something, you let him or her have it. *Give your friend the bat so she can play baseball.*

glad

If you are **glad**, you are happy about something. *I'm glad the sun is shining.*

glass
(glasses)
1. **Glass** is a hard, smooth material that you can see through, such as a window. 2. A **glass** is something you drink from. In a clear **glass**, you can see liquids such as water, milk, and juice.

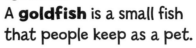

glasses
People wear **glasses** over their eyes to help them see better. **Glasses** are pieces of special glass inside of a frame that fits over the nose.

globe
A **globe** is a big round map of the whole world that spins around.

glove
A **glove** keeps your hand warm and clean. **Gloves** come in pairs and fit over your fingers.

glue
Glue is a thick liquid that helps stick things together. **Glue** gets hard when it dries.

go
(goes, went, gone, going)
When you **go**, you move from one place to another. *The train is **going** down the track.*

goldfish
(goldfish)
A **goldfish** is a small fish that people keep as a pet.

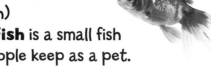

golf
You play the game of **golf** by hitting a little white ball into a hole with a club. A person who plays **golf** is a golfer.

good
(better, best)
1. You are **good** at something you do well. 2. If something tastes really **good**, you will like it. 3. You become healthy or strong if you eat something **good** for you. 4. If you are well behaved and do as you are told, you are **good**.

good-bye
You say **good-bye** when you leave someone or they go away from you.

gorilla
A **gorilla** is a large, hairy ape that lives in Africa.

grandfather
Your **grandfather** is the father of your mother or father.

grandmother

Your **grandmother** is the mother of your mother or father.

grape

A **grape** is a small, round, soft, juicy fruit that grows in bunches on vines. **Grapes** can be purple, green, red, or white.

grass

(grasses)

Grass is a plant with thin, pointy green leaves. **Grass** grows on lawns and fields.

gray

When you mix black and white together, you make the color **gray**. *An elephant is gray.*

green

If you mix yellow and blue together, you make the color **green**. *Grass is green.*

green bean

A **green bean** is a long, thin vegetable.

grin

(grins, grinned, grinning)

When you **grin**, you smile and show your teeth.

group

A **group** is a number of people or things that are gathered together in one place. *A group of children visits the zoo.*

grow

(grows, grew, grown, growing)

To **grow** is to get bigger. *If you water the plant, it will grow.*

guitar

A **guitar** is a musical instrument with strings you touch with your fingers to make a sound.

gum

1. **Gum** is a sweetened stick or tablet you put in your mouth and chew.
2. Your **gums** are the soft flesh in your mouth that surround your teeth.

gym

A **gym** is a big room where people like to exercise and play games such as basketball.

hair

Hair grows on the top of your head. An animal's **hair** is called fur.

half

(halves)

One **half** is one of two pieces of something that are exactly the same size. *My father cut the sandwich in **half**.*

Halloween

Halloween is a holiday that happens on October 31. People dress up in costumes and go door-to-door to get **Halloween** candy.

hammer

A **hammer** is a tool with a long handle and a heavy head. You pound nails into wood with a **hammer** to build things.

hand

(hands, handed, handing)

1. When you **hand** something to somebody, you give it to them with your **hand**. 2. Your **hand** is the part of your body at the end of your arms with four fingers and a thumb.

hand

Hanukkah

Hanukkah is an eight-day Jewish holiday that occurs in the winter. Each night of **Hanukkah**, candles are lit on the menorah. Children play with a dreidel during **Hanukkah**.

happy

(happier, happiest)

If you are **happy**, you feel really good about something. *You are **happy** you won the game of checkers.*

hard

(harder, hardest)

1. If something is **hard**, you cannot easily shape it with your hands or cut it. *A rock is very **hard**.* 2. If something is **hard** to do, it can be difficult. *It is **hard** to learn to tie my shoelaces.*

hat

A **hat** is something you wear on your head.

have

(has, had, having)

1. **Have** means you or other people get or own something. *You **have** a loose tooth.* 2. **Have** means something must be done. *Now that the children are feeling better, they **have** to go to school today.*

he

He is a word you use when you are talking about a boy, a man, or a male animal of any age.

head

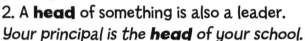
head

1. Your **head** is the part of your body above your neck that has your eyes and mouth in it.
2. A **head** of something is also a leader. *Your principal is the **head** of your school.*

hear

(hears, heard, hearing)
When you **hear** sounds, you notice them with your ears.

heart

1. Your **heart** is inside your chest and pumps blood to all parts of your body. 2. A **heart** is a shape that people enjoy drawing around Valentine's Day.

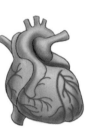

heat

(heats, heated, heating)
When you **heat** something, you make it hot. *Your mom **heats** soup for your lunch.*

heavy

(heavier, heaviest)
Something that weighs a lot is **heavy**. *The box of stones is **heavy**.*

hello

Hello is a way to greet people. You say "**hello**" when you answer your telephone.

helmet

A **helmet** is a hard hat that you wear to protect your head.

help

(helps, helped, helping)
If you **help** someone, you do something useful for them. *You **help** pick up the dishes after dinner.*

hen

A **hen** is a mother chicken, or a female bird that lays eggs.

her

Her means that something is about or belongs to a girl or a woman. *That is **her** gold necklace.*

hers

Hers means something belongs to her, a girl or a woman. *The dress is **hers**.*

hide

(hides, hid, hidden, hiding)
1. If you **hide**, you go where no one can see you. 2. If you **hide** something, you place it where no one can find it.

him

Him means that something is about a boy or a man. *The boy asked his mother to give **him** a quarter.*

hip

Your **hip** is the part of your body on your side just below your waist.

hip

his

His means that something belongs to **him**, a boy or a man. *The toy truck is **his**.*

hit

(hits, hit, hitting)
When you push or touch someone or something very hard, you **hit** that person or thing.

hog

A **hog** is a full-grown pig that farmers raise for its meat, such as ham.

holiday

A **holiday** is a special time when people do not go to school or work. People have parades on some **holidays**, such as New Year's Day.

home

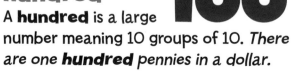

A **home** is the place where you live. A **home** can be a house or an apartment.

homework

Homework is school studies to be done outside of school, usually at home. *The boy is reading a book in his bedroom for **homework.***

honey

Honey is a thick, sweet, liquid food made by bees.

horse

A **horse** is a big animal with long legs and a long tail. People like to ride on a **horse** or in a cart pulled behind a **horse**.

hot

(hotter, hottest)
Hot means very warm. If something is **hot**, such as an oven, it can burn you.

hour

An **hour** is an amount of time. There are 60 minutes in one **hour** and 24 **hours** in one day.

house

A **house** is a building where people, often a single family, live.

hundred

A **hundred** is a large number meaning 10 groups of 10. *There are one **hundred** pennies in a dollar.*

100

I

I means the person who is speaking. *"**I** want to play with the toys."*

ice

Ice is hard, cold, frozen water.

ice cream

Ice cream is a cold, sweet food made from milk that comes in many flavors. You can eat **ice cream** in a cone or a dish.

idea

An **idea** is something that you think of. *Do you have an **idea** how to color Easter eggs?*

if

If means in the event that. *The girl can go to the party **if** her mother lets her.*

igloo

An **igloo** is a house made of blocks of snow or ice.

ill

When you are **ill**, you do not feel very well. *You should stay in bed when you are **ill**.*

important

If something is very **important**, it matters a great deal. *It is **important** to brush your teeth after eating.*

in

In is used to tell about location. *The horse is **in** the barn.*

inch
(inches)

An **inch** is a unit of measure that tells about length. *Most rulers have 12 **inches**.*

insect

An **insect** is a small animal with six legs. Some **insects** can fly. Ants, butterflies, and bees are **insects**.

inside

If you are **inside** of something, it is all around you. *The pear is **inside** the box.*

instead

Instead means in place of something. *I'd rather go by bus **instead** of by train.*

instrument

1. You can use an **instrument** to make music. Pianos, drums, and violins are musical **instruments**.
2. An instrument is anything you use to do something. *At the doctor's office, the doctor used **instruments** to find out why you felt sick.*

into

Into means to go to the inside of something. *Your dog stepped **into** his doghouse.*

iron

1. A hot **iron** is a tool that you use to take wrinkles out of clothes. An **iron** has a handle and a flat side. 2. **Iron** is a very strong metal.

is

(be, am, are, was, were, been, being)
Is means something or someone exists. *The woman **is** a doctor.*

island

An **island** is a piece of land with water all around it. An **island** is smaller than a continent.

it

1. **It** means that one. *I picked **it** up.*
2. In a game of tag, **it** is the player who tries to catch the others.

its

Its means that it relates to that one. ***Its** tail is black and white.*

A B C D E F G H I J K L M N O P Q R S T U V W X Y Z

January

January is the first month of the year. *New Year's Day is in **January**.*

jacket

A **jacket** is a short coat. *You wear a **jacket** when the weather is cool.*

jar

A **jar** is a wide-mouth glass bottle that holds things, such as food, liquid, or coins.

jeans

Jeans are pants made out of a strong denim cloth. **Jeans** are usually blue and have pockets.

jack-in-the-box

(jack-in-the-boxes)
Music plays when you turn the handle of a **jack-in-the-box.** When the music stops, a doll pops out of the toy **jack-in-the-box.**

jelly

(jellies)
Jelly is a soft food made with fruit juice and sugar. *People like to spread **jelly** and peanut butter on bread.*

jack-o-lantern

A **jack-o-lantern** is a Halloween pumpkin. People carve scary or happy faces on their **jack-o-lanterns.**

jelly bean

A **jelly bean** is a small, sweet, chewy, colorful candy.

jam

(jams, jammed, jamming)
1. If something **jams**, it becomes stuck so it is hard to move. 2. **Jam** is a sweet food made by cooking fruit with sugar. You eat **jam** on your toast.

jet

A **jet** is the fastest kind of airplane.
A **jet** has a strong engine.

jewelry

Jewelry is a beautiful decoration that people wear, like rings, earrings, and necklaces.

job

1. A **job** is the work people do to make money. *Daddy has a job as a teacher.*
2. A **job** is something that must be done. *My job is to set the table.*

joke

A **joke** is something you do or say to make others laugh.

juice

Juice is a liquid that you squeeze from fruits, like oranges and grapes. *Juice is good to drink.*

July

July is the seventh month of the year. **July** is a summer month. *People celebrate the Fourth of July with parades and fireworks.*

jump

(jumps, jumped, jumping)
You **jump** when you push yourself up into the air with your legs. *A rabbit jumps with its back legs.*

jump rope

A **jump rope** is a toy with two handles and a rope in between. You swing the **jump rope** over your head and jump when it reaches your feet.

June

June is the sixth month of the year. *People graduate or finish school for the summer in June.*

jungle

A **jungle** is a thick forest in a hot country where many kinds of plants and animals live.

Jupiter

Jupiter is a faraway planet that moves around the sun. **Jupiter** is the largest planet in the solar system.

kangaroo

A **kangaroo** is a large wild animal that jumps with its strong back legs. A mother **kangaroo** carries her baby in front in a pocket.

keep

(keeps, kept, keeping)
1. If you **keep** something, it is safe and you are not giving it away. 2. If you **keep** doing something, you do it over and over again. *I **keep** blowing on the soup to make it cool.* 3. **Keep** means to stay the same way. ***Keep** still so the bee doesn't sting you.*

keeper

A **keeper** cares for someone or something. *An animal **keeper** watches over the animals.*

ketchup

Ketchup is a thick, red liquid food made from tomatoes. *People pour **ketchup** from a bottle on top of hamburgers.*

key

A **key** is a piece of metal that you put in a lock to open or close it. *You can open your door with a **key**.*

kick

(kicks, kicked, kicking)
When you **kick** something, you strike it with your foot.

kid

1. A **kid** is a child. 2. A **kid** is what a young goat is called.

kill

(kills, killed, killing)
To **kill** means to make something or someone die. *You will **kill** your plant if you don't give it water.*

kind

(kinder, kindest)
1. A **kind** of something means a type or sort of thing. *An apple is a **kind** of fruit.* 2. If you are a **kind** person, it means you are nice and helpful.

king

A **king** is a man who rules a country. *The king and queen rode in the royal carriage.*

kiss

(kisses, kissed, kissing)
When you **kiss** someone, your lips touch that person in a nice way.

kitchen

A **kitchen** is a room where people cook food. A **kitchen** has a stove, a refrigerator, and a sink.

kite

A **kite** is a toy that flies in the wind, made from sticks, string, and cloth, paper, or plastic. You hold the string to fly the **kite.**

kitten

A **kitten** is a baby cat with soft fur and little whiskers.

knee

Your **knee** is the part in the middle of your leg that bends.

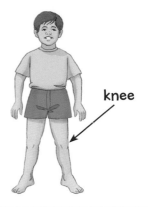

knee

knife

(knives)
A **knife** is a tool with a sharp metal blade and a long handle. *You can cut food into pieces with a knife.*

knock

(knocks, knocked, knocking)
When you **knock,** you hit something hard. *The boy knocked on the door with his hand.*

know

(knows, knew, known, knowing)
1. If you **know** somebody, you have met them before. 2. If you **know** something, it is in your mind. *You know how old you are.*

Kwanza

Kwanza is an African American holiday that celebrates harvest.

A B C D E F G H I J K L M N O P Q R S T U V W X Y Z

ladder

A **ladder** is a set of steps that lets you climb up to and down from tall places. *A firefighter uses a **ladder** to reach a high building.*

lady

(ladies)

A **lady** is a woman.

ladybug

A **ladybug** is a small, round insect that flies. A **ladybug** is often red with black spots.

lake

A **lake** is a lot of water with land all around it.

lamb

A **lamb** is a baby sheep. A **lamb** has soft white or black wool.

large

(larger, largest)

Someone or something that is **large** is very big. *A dinosaur was a **large** animal.*

late

(later, latest)

If you arrive some place after the time you were supposed to arrive there, you are **late.**

laugh

(laughs, laughed, laughing)

When you **laugh,** you make sounds that show you think something funny is happening.

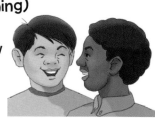

leaf

(leaves)

A **leaf** is a thin, flat part that grows on a plant. *Usually, green **leaves** make the food the plant needs.*

leave

(leaves, left, leaving)

1. When you **leave** a place, you go away from it. *You must **leave** your room to take a bath in the tub.* 2. If you **leave** something somewhere, you go away without it. *You **left** your backpack behind on the school bus.*

leg

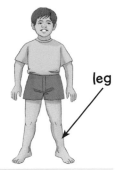

Your **leg** is the long part of your body that you stand and walk on.

leg

lemon

A **lemon** is a yellow fruit with a thick skin. The juice of the **lemon** tastes sour.

let

(lets, let, letting)

If someone **lets** you do something, you are allowed to do it. *Your parents **let** you sleep over at your friend's house.*

lettuce

Lettuce is a vegetable with big green leaves. Many salads are made with **lettuce** leaves.

library

(libraries)

A **library** is a place where books are kept. People can borrow books from the public **library.**

lie

(lies, lay, lain, lied, lying)

1. When you **lie** somewhere, you rest with your body flat on something. *The baby **lies** down in the crib.* 2. A **lie** is something that is not true. *I **lied** when I said I was as tall as a house!*

lift

(lifts, lifted, lifting)

If you **lift** something, you pick it up. *You **lift** up your little brother so he can see above the table.*

light

(lights, lit, lighting)

1. When you **light** something, you make it burn. *They **lit** the birthday candles.* 2. **Light** comes from the sun, lamps, and candles and helps you see. 3. If a color is **light**, it is not very dark. *Pink is a **light** color.* 4. If something is **light**, it is not heavy, and it is easy to lift. *A balloon is very **light**.*

lightning

Lightning is a bright flash of light and electricity you see in the sky when there is a thunderstorm. Sometimes **lightning** hits the ground.

like

(likes, liked, liking)

1. If you **like** something, you enjoy it. *I **like** eating pizza.* 2. When something is **like** something else, it is similar to it, or a match. *His hat looks **like** his brother's hat.*

lime

A **lime** is a sour-tasting, green fruit.

A B C D E F G H I J K L M N O P Q R S T U V W X Y Z

lion

A **lion** is a big wild animal in the cat family with light brown fur and a long tail. The male **lion** has thick hair around its head called a mane.

lip

Your two **lips** are around the outside of your mouth. *You make a curve with your **lips** when you smile.*

listen

(listens, listened, listening)
When you **listen** to someone, you try to hear what she is saying. *He **listened** on the telephone.*

little

(littler, littlest)
When something is **little**, it is small. *A ladybug is a **little** beetle.*

live

(lives, lived, living)
1. If someone or something **lives,** that person or thing is alive. *The cat eats mice to **live**.* 2. If you **live** somewhere, that is where your home is. *Grandma and Grandpa **live** by the lake.*

lizard

A **lizard** is a small, scaly animal with a long body and a long tail. A **lizard** uses its long tongue to catch and eat flies.

log

A **log** is a long piece of wood cut from the trunk of a tree. Some **logs** are burned in fireplaces.

long

(longer, longest)
1. Something that is **long** has a large distance from one end to the other. *A lion has a **long** tail.* 2. **Long** means something lasts for more than a short time. *Night seems to last for a **long** time.*

look

(looks, looked, looking)
You **look** with your eyes to see something.

loud

(louder, loudest)
When something is **loud**, it makes a lot of noise. *A drum is a **loud** instrument.*

love

(loves, loved, loving)
If you **love** someone, you like that person very, very much. *I **love** my baby sister and give her lots of hugs.*

low

(lower, lowest)
If something is **low**, it is near the ground. *The baby crawls **low** on the floor.*

M

machine

A **machine** is something with parts that move together to do a job, such as a car or bicycle.

mad

(madder, maddest)

When you are **mad**, you are very angry. *I am very mad that my friend knocked down my blocks.*

magic

Magic is a special way to do tricks that makes impossible things look real.

magnet

A **magnet** is a piece of metal that other metals stick to. *A magnet picks up pins.*

mail

The **mail** is letters and packages that you send to or get from other people. *You can get your mail at the post office.*

mailbox

(mailboxes)

A **mailbox** holds letters at your house. You can also mail letters by dropping them into a **mailbox** on the street.

makeup

People put **makeup** on their faces to add color to their lips, cheeks, eyes, and mouth. *Lipstick is a kind of makeup.*

man

(men)

When a boy grows up, he becomes a **man**. *My daddy is a man.*

mango

(mangoes)

A **mango** is a yellowish-red fruit that tastes sweet and juicy.

many

(more, most)

Many means a large number of something. *Many ants came to our picnic.*

map

A **map** is a drawing that shows you where different places are, like towns, rivers, and roads.

A B C D E F G H I J K L **M** N O P Q R S T U V W X Y Z

March

March is the third month of the year. *St. Patrick's Day is always **March** 17.*

Mars

Mars, called the red planet, is a little more than half the size of Earth. **Mars** is the fourth planet from the Sun in the solar system.

marshmallow

A **marshmallow** is a soft, white, chewy food. *People roast **marshmallows** over campfires.*

mat

A **mat** is a small rug. *We put a welcome **mat** near the front door for people to wipe their feet on.*

match

(matches, matched, matching)
1. If things **match**, they are alike in some way. *The brown socks **match** the brown shoes.* 2. A **match** is a thin stick you strike to make a fire. 3. A **match** is a game between two players or teams. *The blue team won the soccer **match**.*

math

People learn about numbers when they study **math**. You use your **math** skills when you count and add numbers together.

May

May is the fifth month of the year. *On **May** Day, children often dance around the maypole.*

maybe

Maybe means perhaps something might happen. ***Maybe** you will be able to go swimming today if it stops raining.*

me

Me means I or myself. *Please give the jump rope to **me**.*

mean

(means, meant, meaning)
1. If you say what something **means**, you explain it. *If we put on our pajamas, this **means** it is almost time for bed.* 2. If you **mean** to do something, you plan to do it. *I **mean** to return your book.* 3. If someone is **mean**, he is not very nice. *That **mean** child hit me.*

meat

Meat is a food that comes from animals. *Beef is the **meat** from a cow.*

meet

(meets, met, meeting)
When you **meet** somebody, you both get together at the same place at the same time.

melon

A **melon** is a sweet, juicy fruit that grows on a vine. Watermelon is one kind of **melon.**

menorah

A **menorah** is a special candlestick that holds candles to help celebrate the Jewish holiday, Hanukkah.

Mercury

Mercury is the smallest planet in the solar system. **Mercury** is the closest planet to the Sun.

metal

Metal is something hard that comes out of the ground such as gold, silver, and iron. *Metal is used to make jewelry, cars, and many other machines.*

middle

The **middle** is the place that is the same length away from all sides of something. *The bird sits right in the **middle** of its cage.*

mile

A **mile** is a measurement of 5,280 feet. *It is five **miles** down the road to the nearest library.*

milk

Milk is a white liquid that is good for you to drink. Babies drink **milk** from their mother or from cows.

minute

A **minute** is a short amount of time. There are 60 **minutes** in one hour.

mirror

A **mirror** is a special glass that reflects an image. *You look into the **mirror** to see yourself.*

miss

(misses, missed, missing)
1. If you **miss** something, like a ball, you did not hit it or catch it. 2. If you **miss** somebody, you are sad because you aren't with him. *I **miss** my dog who ran away.*

mistake

If you make a **mistake**, you do something wrong. *I left the ice cream out of the freezer and let it melt by **mistake**.*

mitten

A **mitten** keeps your hand warm. A **mitten** has one place for your thumb and another space for all your fingers together.

Monday

Monday is the first day of the week after the weekend.

A B C D E F G H I J K L M N O P Q R S T U V W X Y Z

money

You use **money**, like coins and bills, to pay for things you buy.

monkey

A **monkey** is an animal with long arms and legs and a long tail. **Monkeys** are good at climbing trees.

monster

A **monster** is a big scary creature in books and movies.

month

A **month**, like January, is part of the year. There are 12 **months** in a year.

moon

The **moon** is the big bright light that you see in the sky at night. The **moon** travels around Earth about once a month.

morning

The **morning** is the early part of the day before noon. The sun rises in the **morning**.

mother

A **mother** is a woman who has a child.

motorcycle

A **motorcycle** is a big bicycle with an engine. One or two people can ride a **motorcycle**, and it can go as fast as a car.

mouse
(mice)

1. A **mouse** is a small, furry animal with a long, thin tail, and sharp teeth. A **mouse** lives in a forest, a field, or a house. 2. A **mouse** is a small piece of equipment you use to move things around a computer screen.

mouth

mouth

Your **mouth** is the part of your face that you use to talk and eat. Your **mouth** opens and closes.

movie

A **movie** is a story told with moving pictures on a big screen or a TV.

muffin

A **muffin** is a small, sweet cake that people like to eat for breakfast. Some **muffins** have nuts or pieces of fruit inside.

multiply
(multiplies, multiplied, multiplying)
When you **multiply** a number, you add it to itself a certain number of times. Two multiplied by five is ten: 2 x 5=10. The sign to **multiply** is x.

music

Music is the sound that comes from playing an instrument, like a horn, or from singing with your voice.

N

nail

1. A **nail** is a short, pointy piece of metal that you hit on its head with a hammer to build something. **Nails** hold things together.
2. Your **nails** are the smooth, shiny, hard ends of your toes and fingers.

name

A **name** is what you call somebody or something.

nap

A **nap** is a short rest. *A puppy takes several naps during the day.*

napkin

A **napkin** is a folded piece of cloth or paper that you use while you eat. People wipe their faces and hands with **napkins**.

nature

Nature is everything on Earth that is not made by people.

near

(nearer, nearest)
If something is **near**, it is not far away. *My neck is near my face.*

neck

Your **neck** joins your shoulders to your head.

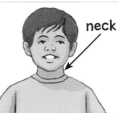

neck

neighbor

A **neighbor** is someone who lives near you.

Neptune

Neptune is the eighth planet from the Sun. **Neptune** is the fourth largest planet in the solar system. Like Earth, **Neptune** orbits around the Sun.

nest

A **nest** is a home that birds and some animals build for their young out of mud, straw, or sticks. Birds lay eggs in **nests**.

net

1. A **net** is pieces of string tied together with holes in between. People catch fish or butterflies in **nets**.
2. A **net** is used with balls in different games, like tennis and soccer. 3. **Net** is another word for the Internet. The **Net** is a system where computers give and receive information.

A B C D E F G H I J K L M N O P Q R S T U V W X Y Z

never

Never means not at any time. *You must **never** play with matches.*

new

(newer, newest)
1. If something is **new**, it has just been made or has not been used. *The girl has **new** shoes.* 2. **New** also means different. *We just moved to a **new** house.*

news

News is information about things that have happened. *Good **news**! My brother is feeling better.*

newspaper

A **newspaper** is many folded sheets of paper with words and pictures on them. You can read about what is happening in the world in the **newspaper.**

next

Next means the one after this one. ***Next** week is my birthday party.*

nice

(nicer, nicest)
If something is **nice**, you feel good about it and like it. *My new haircut is very **nice**.*

nickel

A **nickel** is a round coin that is worth five cents.

night

Night is the time of day when the sun goes down and it is dark. People sleep at night.

nine

Nine is a number that means one more than eight. 8+1=9.

nineteen

Nineteen is a number that is one more than eighteen. 18+1=19.

ninety

Ninety is a number ten less than one hundred. **Ninety** is nine sets of ten.
10+10+10+10+10+10+10+10+10=90.

no

1. **No** means not any. *There are **no** more peanuts left.* 2. **No** means not so. ***No**, I did not break the glass.* 3. **No** means that you do not have permission. ***No**, you cannot have some candy.*

nobody
Nobody means no one. **Nobody** wanted to eat spinach for dinner.

nod
(nods, nodded, nodding)
When you **nod** your head, it moves up and down. You can **nod** your head to mean yes.

noise
A **noise** is a sound that someone or something makes. *The dog's bark is a loud noise.*

none
None means not any. *After we ate all the bananas, there were **none** left.*

north
North is a direction. The needle points to **north** on the compass.

nose
Your **nose** is a part of your face that helps you to smell and breathe.

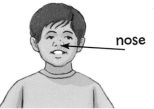

nose

not
Not makes something negative. *My aunt is **not** happy about her missing necklace.*

notebook
A **notebook** has pages for you to write or draw on.

nothing
Nothing means not at all or of no importance. *Your spilled water is **nothing**. We will clean it up.*

November
November is a month in the fall of the year. *Thanksgiving is a holiday in **November**.*

number
A **number** is a word or sign that says how many things you have. *The symbol 5 means the **number** five.*

nurse
A **nurse** is someone who takes care of sick or hurt people. **Nurses** work in hospitals and doctors' offices.

nut
A **nut** is a seed or fruit that has a hard shell. People crack the shell and eat **nuts** such as cashews and almonds.

A B C D E F G H I J K L M N O P Q R S T U V W X Y Z

O

oar

An **oar** is a long piece of wood with one flat end. You push the **oar** to row a boat through the water.

oboe

An **oboe** is a long, thin musical instrument. You blow into the **oboe** to make sounds.

ocean

An **ocean** is a very big sea. The water in the **ocean** tastes salty.

October

October is a month in the fall of the year. *Halloween is a holiday in October.*

octopus

(octopuses)
An **octopus** is a sea animal with eight long arms.

off

1. **Off** means away from something. *The ball fell off the shelf.* 2. **Off** is the opposite of on. *My brother turned the television off so we could eat dinner.*

office

An **office** is a place where people work. An **office** has a desk, a chair, and maybe a computer.

officer

An **officer** is an important person who is in charge of other people. A police **officer** and an army **officer** make sure people follow the rules.

often

If you do something **often**, you do it a lot of times. *We often go to the fast-food restaurant to eat.*

oil

Oil is a thick, slippery liquid. Light **oil** that comes from plants is used for cooking. Dark **oil** that comes from the ground helps heat your home and make your car run.

OK

OK, or **okay**, means that things are all right. *It's **OK** that you go to play at your friend's house.*

old

(older, oldest)
1. If someone or something is **old**, they have lived or been around for a long time. *My grandpa is old at 90.*
2. **Old** means something that you had before. *That looks like my **old** shirt.*

olive

An **olive** is a green or brown vegetable that grows on trees. People eat **olives** in salad and on pizza.

on

1. **On** means atop something. *The bowl is **on** the table.* 2. **On** is the opposite of off. *Turn the light **on** so we can see.*

once

1. **Once** means only one time. *We went to the zoo **once**.* 2. **Once** means as soon as or after. *You can watch TV **once** you have finished picking up all your toys.*

one

One is a number. **One** comes before two.

onion

An **onion** is a round vegetable with a papery skin. An **onion** has a strong taste and smell.

only

Only means a limited amount. *You can **only** have one piece of watermelon.*

open

(opens, opened, opening)
1. If you take a lid off something, you **open** it. 2. If something is **open**, you can go through it. *They walked through the open door.*

or

Or means there is a choice of some kind. *You can pick apples **or** oranges.*

orange

1. **Orange** is a bright color. A pumpkin is **orange**. 2. An **orange** is a sweet, round fruit with an **orange**-colored skin. People squeeze **oranges** to get juice.

organ

1. An **organ** is a musical keyboard instrument like a piano. The music from an **organ** comes out of long pipes.
2. An **organ** is a part of your body that helps you to live, such as your lungs in your chest.

ornament

An **ornament** is a special decoration to make things look pretty. *You can put a Christmas **ornament** on a tree.*

other

Other means different than the one you have. *Where is your **other** pencil?*

our

Our means it has to do with or belongs to us. *It is **our** picnic basket.*

out

1. **Out** means away from the inside. *The cat climbed **out** of the box.* 2. **Out** means to get rid of. *The forest ranger has put **out** the campfire.*

outside

Outside means not in something. *The pear is **outside** the box.*

oven

An **oven** is the hot inside part of the stove where you cook food. **Ovens** have doors that close to keep the heat inside.

over

1. **Over** means across something. *The turtle crawled **over** the path.* 2. If someone tells you something **over**, they tell it to you again. *Why must I tell you over and **over** to wear your mittens outside?* 3. **Over** means that something is finished. *When one team wins, the football game is **over**.*

owl

An **owl** is a bird with large, round eyes that are good for seeing small animals at night. An **owl** makes a hooting sound.

own

(owns, owned, owning)
If you **own** something, it belongs to you. *I **own** the lion mask.*

pacifier

A **pacifier** has a little rubber end for a baby to suck on. A **pacifier** comforts a crying baby.

page

A **page** is a piece of paper inside a book.

pail

A **pail** is a container used to carry things like water from place to place. A **pail** has a handle and a flat bottom.

paint

(paints, painted, painting)
1. You can use brushes and paints to **paint** or make a colorful picture.
2. When you **paint** a wall or house, you put **paint** on it.
3. **Paint** is a liquid that you can use to put color in pictures or on houses.

painting

A **painting** is a picture that someone has painted with a brush.

pan

A **pan** is a metal dish with a handle. You cook food in a **pan**. *My brother cooked eggs in a frying pan on top of the stove.*

pancake

A **pancake** is a thin, round cake made with flour, eggs, and milk. *After you cook the pancake, you put butter and syrup on top and then eat it.*

panda

A **panda** is a huge black-and-white, furry animal that looks like a bear. **Pandas** live in China.

pants

Pants are clothes that cover the bottom half of your body. **Pants** have two legs and, sometimes, pockets.

papaya

A **papaya** is a fruit with a sweet, yellow inside and yellow, pink, or orange skin. **Papayas** grow on trees in places with warm weather.

paper

Paper is a thin sheet made from cloth or wood. People write and draw on **paper** and wrap things in it, too.

A B C D E F G H I J K L M N O P Q R S T U V W X Y Z

party
(parties)

When a group of friends get together to eat and have fun, they have a **party.** *You eat cake at a birthday* **party.**

pat
(pats, patted, patting)

When you **pat** something, you tap it gently with your fingers or hand.

pay
(pays, paid, paying)

When you **pay** someone, you give that person money for something. *He* **paid** *the lady for the papaya.*

pea

A **pea** is a small, round, green vegetable that grows inside a long pod.

peace

Peace is a quiet time without any fighting between people.

peach
(peaches)

A **peach** is a soft, juicy fruit with a pit inside and yellow-red, fuzzy skin outside.

peanut

A **peanut** is a seed from a plant. **Peanuts** become ripe under the ground. The small oval **peanuts** found inside a brown shell are roasted before you eat them. Although some people believe **peanuts** are nuts, they are really more like beans or peas.

peanut butter

Peanut butter is a soft food made from peanuts. You spread sticky **peanut butter** on sandwiches and crackers.

pear

A **pear** is a yellow, green, or brown fruit that is sweet and juicy. One end of the round **pear** is bigger than the other.

pecan

A **pecan** is a nut with a smooth shell that grows on trees. People enjoy eating **pecan** pie.

pen

A **pen** is a long, thin tool filled with ink for writing or drawing.

pencil

A **pencil** is a long, thin stick with graphite in the middle. The dark point of a **pencil** makes marks when drawing or writing.

penguin

A **penguin** is a large black-and-white bird that swims in the sea but does not fly. **Penguins** live where it is very cold.

penny

(pennies)

A **penny**, or one cent, is a coin. A **penny** is the smallest amount of money in the United States and Canada.

pepper

1. **Pepper** is a black spicy powder to put on food.
2. A **pepper** is a bright green, yellow, or red vegetable. *I like **peppers** on my pizza.*

person

(people)

A **person** is a man, a woman, or a child.

pet

A **pet** is an animal, like a dog or cat, that you take care of in your home. People usually give their **pets** names.

phone

Phone is short for *telephone.* A **phone** is a machine that lets you talk and listen to others. Part of the **phone** has numbers for you to push or dial to reach someone.

photograph

A **photograph** is a picture you take with a camera. A **photograph** might be printed in black and white or in color.

piano

A **piano** is a large musical instrument with black keys and white keys that you tap with your fingers to make sounds.

pie

A **pie** has a crispy crust over a thick filling of fruit, meat, or vegetables. A **pie** is baked in the oven.

pig

A **pig** is a fat farm animal with short legs and a curly tail. *A **pig** squeals, oink, oink!*

pigeon

A **pigeon** is a bird whose small head bobs up and down when it walks. **Pigeons** like to sit on statues and rooftops.

piglet

A **piglet** is a baby pig with pink skin. **Piglets** sleep together next to their mother.

pillow

A **pillow** is a bag filled with soft material, like feathers. You rest your head on a **pillow** to go to sleep in bed.

pilot

A **pilot** is someone who flies an airplane. A **pilot** sits in the front of the plane with the controls.

piñata

A **piñata** is a decorated hollow Mexican toy filled with candy and gifts. Children try to break a hanging **piñata** with a stick so the treats will fall out.

pineapple

A **pineapple** is a yellow-brown fruit with sharp, pointed green leaves on the top. The inside of the **pineapple** is yellow, very juicy, and sweet.

pinecone

Sometimes scaly and sticky, a **pinecone** is something that grows on evergreen trees. **Pinecone** seeds grow into new trees.

pink

When you mix white and red together, you make the color **pink.** *Baby pigs are* **pink**.

piranha

A **piranha** is a fish in South America with very sharp teeth. **Piranhas** swim in groups to find a meal.

pitcher

A **pitcher** is like a big cup with a handle used to store a lot of liquid. You can pour juice or milk from a special opening at the top of a **pitcher.**

pizza

A **pizza** is a flat, round food baked in a very hot oven. You can add tomato sauce, cheese, and other toppings to the **pizza** crust.

plane

A **plane** is a big machine that flies. **Plane** is short for *airplane*.

plant

A **plant** is a living thing that grows in dirt or water. Most **plants**, like trees and flowers, have roots, stems, leaves, flowers, and seeds.

plate

A **plate** is a round, flat object that you put food on. *You put cake on a dessert* **plate**.

play
(plays, played, playing)
1. When you **play**, you have fun. *I play catch with my friend.* 2. If you **play** a musical instrument, you make sounds with it. *My fingers play the piano.* 3. A **play** is a story you act out or watch. *I am Snow White in the school play.*

please
Please is a word you use when you ask for something in a nice way. *Would you please make me a sandwich?*

plum
A **plum** is a juicy fruit with smooth green, purple, red, or yellow skin. A **plum** is soft and yellow inside with a big pit.

plumber
A **plumber** is a person who works on water pipes and water machines. A **plumber** fixes a leak in your sink.

plus
You use the word **plus** when you add numbers together. The sign for **plus** is +. *One plus three equals four: 1+3=4.*

police
Police are people whose job it is to keep others safe and stop them from breaking the laws. Many **police** officers wear special badges and uniforms.

pony
(ponies)
A **pony** is a small horse that children like to ride. **Ponies** can pull carts.

popcorn
Hard **popcorn** seeds burst open and puff out when you heat them. Cooked **popcorn** is white, fluffy, crunchy, and good to eat for a snack!

porcupine
A **porcupine** is an animal with stiff pointed hairs, called quills, on its back. A **porcupine** sticks its quills into an animal that gets too close.

possible
If something is **possible**, it can be done. *If I hold your hand, it is possible for me to stand on one foot.*

pot
A **pot** is a deep, round pan used for cooking things like soup. A **pot** has one or two handles and a lid.

potato
(potatoes)
A **potato** is a round vegetable that grows underground with brown or red skin. You can boil, fry, mash, and bake **potatoes**.

pour

(pours, poured, pouring)
When you **pour** something, it flows out of the container. *The child **pours** the water from the pitcher.*

present

1. A **present** is something you give someone for a special reason. *I gave my friend a birthday **present**.*
2. The **present** time is now. *At **present**, all of the ducks are quacking.*

president

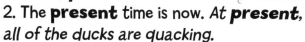

A **president** is an important person who others have picked to lead a country or organization.

press

(presses, pressed, pressing)
When you **press** something, you push on it. *You **press** the letters on your computer keyboard.*

prince

A **prince** is the son of the king or queen. A **prince** lives in a palace.

princess

(princesses)
A **princess** is the daughter of the king or queen. A **princess** lives in a palace.

print

(prints, printed, printing)
When people **print** words and pictures, they put them on paper with a pencil, a pen, or a machine.

pull

(pulls, pulled, pulling)
When you move someone or something toward you, you **pull** it. *You **pull** on the oar to row the boat.*

pumpkin

A **pumpkin** is a large, round orange fruit that you can cook and make into **pumpkin** pies. *People carve faces in **pumpkins** for Halloween.*

puppy

(puppies)
A **puppy** is a young dog. **Puppies** like to play and chew on things.

purple

When you mix red and blue, you make the color **purple**. *A **plum** is purple.*

puzzle

A **puzzle** is a game, toy, or question that you have fun trying to figure out. *How do I put this **puzzle** together?*

Q

quart

A **quart** is a measure for liquids, such as milk. There are four **quarts** in a gallon.

quarter

1. A **quarter** is one of four equal parts of something. *You can have a* **quarter** *of the pizza.*
2. A **quarter** is a silver coin. One **quarter** is the same value as 25 pennies.

queen

A **queen** is a woman who rules a country. A **queen** is sometimes married to a king.

question

You ask a **question** when you want to find out about something. *My teacher had a good answer to my* **question**.

quick

(quicker, quickest)
1. If someone moves fast, he is **quick**.
2. **Quick** also means something must be done in a short time.

quiet

(quieter, quietest)
If someone is **quiet**, she doesn't make any noise. *Be* **quiet** *in the library.*

quilt

A **quilt** is two pieces of cloth stuffed with soft material and sewn together. People sew pretty designs on **quilts** and use them for a warm bed cover.

quit

(quits, quit, quitting)
If you **quit** something, you stop doing it. *I* **quit** *playing soccer because I broke my foot when I fell.*

quiz

(quizzes)
A **quiz** is a short test that asks questions to find out how much you know. *My teacher gave me a* **quiz** *to see if I could spell animal names.*

rabbit

A **rabbit** is a small, wild, furry animal with long ears. A **rabbit** moves by hopping. **Rabbits** like to eat carrots.

raccoon

A **raccoon** is a furry animal with a long, ringed tail and a black fur mask around its eyes. A **raccoon** sleeps in the day and looks for food at night.

radio

A **radio** is a machine that picks up waves in the air and turns them into sounds.

rain

Rain is small drops of water that fall to the ground from clouds in the sky.

rainbow

A **rainbow** is a curved band of colors you sometimes see in the sky when the sun shines after the rain.

raisin

A **raisin** is a small dried grape. Chewy and sweet, **raisins** are good in cereal or for a snack.

rake

A **rake** is a tool with a long handle and big teeth that you use to collect leaves and grass outdoors.

Ramadan

Ramadan is the ninth month of the Islamic year. During **Ramadan,** people do not eat between dawn and sunset.

raspberry

(raspberries)

A **raspberry** is a small, bumpy, black or red fruit with many tiny seeds. **Raspberries** grow on bushes.

rat

A **rat** is an animal that looks like a big mouse with a long, thin tail and very sharp teeth. A **rat** makes a *squeak, squeak* sound.

ray

A **ray** is a thin beam of light. *A **ray** from the flashlight shines through the night.*

read

(reads, read, reading)
When you **read**, you look at words and know what they mean.

rectangle

A **rectangle** is a shape with two long sides, two short sides, and four corners. *A door is a **rectangle**.*

red

Red is a color. *Fire engines and cherries are **red** things.*

referee

A **referee** is a person who makes sure the players follow the rules at games such as football and basketball.

refrigerator

A **refrigerator** is a machine that keeps food cold and fresh. The coldest part of the **refrigerator** is the freezer.

remember

(remembers, remembered, remembering)
If you **remember** something, you keep it in your mind. *I **remembered** to get the cake out of the oven.*

reptile

A **reptile** is an animal that has cold blood and skin with scales on it. **Reptiles**, such as snakes and turtles, lay eggs.

rescue

(rescues, rescued, rescuing)
If you **rescue** somebody, you help them or save them from danger. *The firefighter **rescued** the cat from the tree.*

rest

(rests, rested, resting)
1. When you **rest**, you stop what you are doing because you are tired. After playing in the park, you need to **rest**.
2. The **rest** is what is left over when a part of something has been taken away. *I will give you the **rest** of the cake.*

rice

Rice is a small white or brown seed that gets soft when you cook it for food. **Rice** grows in wet land in hot countries.

rich

(richer, richest)
If someone is **rich,** that person has a lot of money or things, like jewelry. *The **rich** man owns five cars.*

ride

(rides, rode, ridden, riding)
To **ride** is to travel in or on something. People may **ride** bikes, horses, buses, or other moving things.

ring

(rings, rang, rung, ringing)
1. If something **rings**, it sounds like a bell.
2. A **ring** is a piece of pretty jewelry you wear on your finger. 3. A **ring** is a circle shape with an empty center. *The children held hands and made a **ring** to play the game.*

river

A **river** is a long, wide bit of water with land on both sides. A **river** flows to the sea.

robin

A **robin** is a songbird with red feathers on its breast.

robot

A **robot** is a machine that does some work that people do. Computerized **robots** can build cars in factories.

rock

(rocks, rocked, rocking)
1. When you **rock** something, you move it back and forth or side to side. *Mommy **rocks** the baby in the **rocking** chair.* 2. A **rock** is a hard stone that comes from the earth. **Rock** rises from the earth as mountains.

rocket

A **rocket** is a tubelike machine that flies very fast and very high. Burning gasses inside the **rocket** make it shoot into space.

roof

A **roof** is the flat or pointed top part of a building that covers it to keep out the rain. Cars and trucks also have a flat **roof** on the top.

roof

A B C D E F G H I J K L M N O P Q R S T U V W X Y Z

room

1. A **room** is a space with walls around it inside a building. *A kitchen is a room.*
2. **Room** also means space. *Is there room for me in the bed?*

rooster

A **rooster**, a male chicken with a fancy tail, lives on a farm. A **rooster** makes a noisy *cock-a-doodle-do* sound.

rose

A **rose** is a sweet-smelling, beautiful flower with sharp points called thorns on its stem. **Roses** grow on bushes.

round

(rounder, roundest)
Something that is **round** has the same shape as a circle or a ball.

row

(rows, rowed, rowing)
1. When you **row** a boat, you move it through the water with oars. 2. A **row** is a line of people or things. *The girl put her teddy bears in a row.*

rowboat

A **rowboat** is something that people sit in to ride through the water. They use two oars to move the **rowboat** along.

rubber band

A **rubber band** is a long circle of stretchy rubber that can slide over things to hold them in place.

rug

A **rug** is a strong, sturdy cloth used to cover a floor.

ruler

1. A **ruler** is a tool that helps you measure how long something is or draw a straight line. 2. A **ruler** is a person who is the leader of the country.

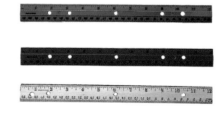

run

(runs, ran, running)
When you **run**, you move your legs very quickly. If you **run**, you go faster than walking.

sad
(sadder, saddest)
If you are **sad**, you feel unhappy. *You are sad that you broke your arm.*

sailor
A **sailor** is someone who works on a ship. **Sailors** keep ships clean and running smoothly.

salad
A **salad** is a cold mixture of fruits, vegetables, or meats. You might eat dressing on top of a **salad**.

salt
Salt is a white powder people put on food for flavor. *Pretzels have salt on them.*

sandwich
(sandwiches)
A **sandwich** is two slices of bread with food, such as meat, cheese, and vegetables, in between.

Santa Claus
Santa Claus is a jolly old man with a round belly who leaves gifts for children on Christmas Eve. **Santa Claus** dresses in a red suit and rides in a sleigh pulled by flying reindeer.

Saturday
Saturday is the seventh day of the week. You do not go to school on **Saturday**, a weekend day.

Saturn
Saturn is a planet in the solar system that is larger than Earth. **Saturn** has rings around it.

saxophone
A **saxophone** is a musical instrument that sounds like a horn. You blow into a **saxophone** and press the keys to change the sounds.

scare
(scares, scared, scaring)
If something **scares** you, you feel afraid. *All the thunder and lightning scared the dog.*

scarf
(scarves)

A **scarf** is a long piece of material you wear around your head or neck to keep warm.

school
School is a place where people go to learn. In **school**, the teacher helps children learn to read, write, and do math.

science
Science is the study of things like animals, plants, and the planets.

scientist

A **scientist** is a person who studies about the world and how it works. A **scientist** might study about one thing, such as the stars.

scissors
A pair of **scissors** is a cutting tool with two sharp, pointed parts joined together. **Scissors** can cut cloth or paper.

sea
A **sea** is a large body of salty water.

seal
(seals, sealed, sealing)

1. If you **seal** something, you close it. I *am sealing this letter shut.* 2. A **seal** is an ocean animal with thick, smooth fur and webbed feet to help it swim. A **seal** makes a barking sound.

seat

A **seat** is a place where you can sit. *Two children sit together on the seat on the school bus.*

seed

A **seed** is a little part of a plant that grows into a new plant if you put it in the ground. Most **seeds** have a hard shell to keep the tiny new plant inside safe. You can eat some **seeds,** like pumpkin **seeds.**

seesaw
A **seesaw** is a big playground toy with a long, flat board. People sit on each end of the **seesaw** to move it up and down.

sell
(sells, sold, selling)
If someone **sells** you something, they give it to you when you pay them money.

sentence

A **sentence** is a group of words that makes a complete thought. A written **sentence** starts with a capital letter and usually ends with a period.

September

September is a month of the year in the fall. *Labor Day is a holiday in **September**.*

seven

Seven is a number that is one more than six. 6+1=7.

seventeen

Seventeen is a number that is one more than sixteen. 16+1=17.

seventy

Seventy is a number that is seven groups of 10. 10+10+10+10+10+10+10=70.

shampoo

Shampoo is a kind of soap you use to wash your hair. When you rub **shampoo** in your hair, it makes bubbles.

shark

A **shark** is a large gray ocean fish with a wide mouth filled with sharp teeth. **Sharks** attack other fish.

sharp

(sharper, sharpest)
If something is **sharp**, it has an edge or a point that is good for cutting. A knife and scissors are tools that are **sharp**.

she

She means a girl or a woman. ***She** is wearing a dress.*

sheep

(sheep)
A **sheep** is a farm animal with thick wool or hair. **Sheep** make a *baaa, baaa* sound.

shell

A **shell** is a hard cover that protects the soft things inside of it. Eggs, nuts, and turtles have **shells**.

shirt

A **shirt** is something you wear on the top part of your body. Most **shirts** have sleeves to cover your arms and buttons down the front.

shoe

A **shoe** is something you wear on your foot to keep it warm or protect it. You slide your foot in and buckle, snap, zip, or tie a **shoe**.

shorts

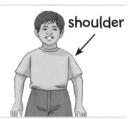

Shorts are pants that usually end above the knees. You wear **shorts** when the weather is warm.

shoulder

shoulder

Your **shoulder** is the highest part of your arm.

shovel

A **shovel** is a digging tool with a long handle on one end and a curved piece on the other end to pick up things. You use a **shovel** to dig a hole in the dirt.

shy

(shier, shiest)

If someone is **shy**, he may feel a little afraid or hold back and not join in right away. *The little boy sat by himself at the party because he was **shy**.*

sick

(sicker, sickest)

When you are **sick**, you do not feel well. *When the baby was **sick**, Daddy took her to the doctor.*

sidewalk

A **sidewalk** is a paved path on the side of a road or going to someone's house. *You can ride on the **sidewalk** with your scooter.*

sign

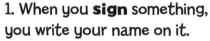

(signs, signed, signing)

1. When you **sign** something, you write your name on it.
2. A **sign** has pictures or words that tell you something. *If you see a red **sign** with the letters* STOP, *you must stop your car.*
3. A **sign** is a shape that means something. *The +* **sign** *means to add things together.*

silly

(sillier, silliest)

If you say or do something that is **silly**, you are being funny. Sometimes, when people don't think carefully about what they are doing, they can be **silly** by accident. *Wearing your shoes on the wrong feet is **silly**.*

sing

(sings, sang, sung, singing)

When you **sing**, you use your voice to make music.

sink

(sinks, sank, sunk, sinking)

1. When you **sink** something, it goes under water. *A heavy rock **sinks** in the water.*
2. A **sink** is a place where you wash things, like dishes or your hands.

sister

A **sister** is a girl who has the same mother or father as you.

sit

(sits, sat, sitting)
When you **sit**, you rest with your bottom on something. *The boy **sits** on the chair.*

six

Six is a number that is one more than five. 5+1=6.

sixteen

Sixteen is a number that is one more than fifteen. 15+1=16.

sixty

Sixty means six groups of ten. 10+10+10+10+10+10=60.

skateboard

A **skateboard** is a low, flat board with wheels on the bottom. You ride a **skateboard** with one foot while pushing the other foot off the ground. *Some **skateboard** riders can spin and jump with the board.*

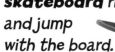

skeleton

A **skeleton** is the set of bones inside your body that connect together and give your body its shape. Your **skeleton** protects your soft insides.

skin

1. **Skin** is what covers the outside of your body. 2. **Skin** is the outside layer of many fruits and vegetables. *You can peel the yellow **skin** of the banana.*

skull

Your **skull** is the round bone of your head that protects your brain.

skunk

A **skunk** is a small wild animal with a long, black-and-white-striped, furry tail. A frightened **skunk** squirts a bad-smelling spray.

sleep

(sleeps, slept, sleeping)
When you **sleep**, you close your eyes and rest your whole body and mind. People usually **sleep** at night in a bed.

slide

(slides, slid, sliding)
1. When something **slides**, it moves along easily. *You just **slide** along on the ice.*
2. A **slide** is a long, smooth ramp that leans against a ladder on the playground. You climb the ladder, sit on the **slide**, then zip down it.

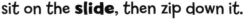

small
(smaller, smallest)
If somebody or something is **small**, it is not very big. *A violet is a **small** plant.*

smart
(smarter, smartest)
Someone who is **smart** is bright and uses her brain to know things. *A **smart** girl does not play with matches.*

smile

(smiles, smiled, smiling)
1. When you **smile**, the corners of your mouth turn up. 2. A **smile** is a look your face makes when you are happy.

snack

A **snack** is a little something you can eat quickly in between meals. A piece of fruit or crackers and cheese are healthy **snacks**.

snake
A **snake** is a long, thin reptile without legs. A **snake** wiggles along by sliding over the ground.

snow

Snow is water that has frozen into tiny pieces and falls from the sky. During very cold weather, white **snow** sometimes covers the ground. *We made the **snow** into snowballs.*

so
So means very or highly. *This soda tastes **so** sweet.*

soap
Soap is something you use with water to wash and clean things, like dishes or your hands. **Soap** comes in bars, liquids, or powders.

soccer
Soccer is a game where two teams try to kick a ball into a big net.

sock
A **sock** is something soft that you wear on your foot under your shoes.

soda
Soda is a sweet drink with fizzy bubbles in it.

A B C D E F G H I J K L M N O P Q R S T U V W X Y Z

soft
(softer, softest)
If something feels **soft**, it is not scratchy or hard. *A pillow is* ***soft***.

softball
In the game of **softball**, one team tries to hit a white ball with a bat while the other team tries to catch it. **Softball** players try to score points by running around the bases.

someone
Someone means somebody or an unnamed person. *I see* ***someone*** *on the skateboard.*

son
A **son** is a boy or a man who is somebody's child.

song
A **song** is a piece of music. Many **songs** have words that you can sing. *The kids are singing a* ***song***.

soon
(sooner, soonest)
If something is happening **soon**, it will happen not very long from now. *The airplane will be taking off very* ***soon***.

sorry
(sorrier, sorriest)
If you feel **sorry**, you are very sad about something that happened. *I am* ***sorry*** *you broke your foot.*

soup
Soup is a hot liquid food. Sometimes **soup** can have meat or vegetables in it. *We had tomato* ***soup*** *with crackers for lunch today.*

south
South is a direction that is on your right side when you watch the sun come up in the morning.

space
1. **Space** is a place with nothing in it. *There is a lot of* ***space*** *inside an empty bag.* 2. **Space** is the huge area that is everything outside Earth. **Space** is where the stars and planets are.

spaghetti
Spaghetti is a long, thin, stringy pasta. People eat **spaghetti** with sauces, like tomato or cheese, on top.

speed
(speeds, sped, speeding)
If someone or something **speeds**, that person or thing is in a big hurry and moves very fast. *The train is **speeding** past the towns.*

spell
(spells, spelled, spelling)
1. When you **spell** a word, you say or write the letters in order. C-A-T **spells** cat. 2. In stories or movies, a **spell** is a set of special words that make magic happen. *The fairy princess said "Hocus Pocus" and put a **spell** on the sleeping cat to make him jump in the air.*

spider
A **spider** is a small creature with eight legs and no wings. A **spider** spins a sticky web to catch other tiny animals for food.

spinach
Spinach is a vegetable that grows in bunches of dark, green leaves. You can eat **spinach** raw or cooked.

sponge
A **sponge** is something soft with little holes in it that cleans up wet spills. You can also wet a **sponge** to wipe away messes.

spoon

A **spoon** is a tool with a long handle and a small round bowl used for eating. You can eat soft or runny food, like ice cream or soup, with a **spoon**.

sport
A **sport** is a game that exercises your body to help it stay healthy. **Sports**, such as baseball or tennis, are played for fun.

spring
(springs, sprang, sprung, springing)
1. If something **springs** out, it jumps. *The tiger **springs** out of the bushes.*
2. **Spring** is the season of the year between winter and summer. Flowers start to bloom in **spring**. 3. A **spring** is a curly piece of metal that pops back into place when you touch it.

square
A **square** is a shape with four straight sides of the same length and four even corners.

squirrel
A **squirrel** is a small gray, brown, black, or red animal with a long fluffy tail. **Squirrels** eat nuts and live in nests they build in trees.

star

1. A **star** is a bright light of burning gas that you see in the sky at night. 2. A **star** is a shape with five or six points. Sometimes your teacher puts a **star** shape on top of your paper if you do a good job. 3. A **star** is someone famous, like a person in movies or TV.

state

(states, stated, stating)
1. If you **state** something, you use words to tell someone about it. 2. A **state** is a small part of a country with its own people, land, and laws. *The **state** of Texas is in the southern part of the United States.*

stem

A **stem** is the long part of a plant that grows out of the ground. Roots, branches, and flowers grow from **stems**.

stem

step

1. A **step** is something you stand on to make you taller to reach things. Many **steps** in a row are called a staircase. 2. When you take a **step**, you lift up your foot and put it down in another place.

sticker

A **sticker** is a gummed label with words, numbers, or pictures, much like a stamp. People collect pretty colored **stickers** and stick them in a book.

still

(stiller, stillest)
1. If someone or something is **still**, it is not moving. *The deer stood **still** in the woods.* 2. If something is **still** happening, it has not yet stopped. *Even though it feels a little warmer, it is **still** snowing outside.*

stomach

Your **stomach** is the place inside of your body where your food goes to digest when you eat it.

stop

(stops, stopped, stopping)
1. If you **stop** what you are doing, you do not do it any more. ***Stop** blowing up the balloon, or it will pop.* 2. If something that is moving **stops**, it stands still. *The car **stopped** for the traffic light.*

stop sign

A **stop sign** is red with the word *STOP* painted on it in white. A **stop sign** is placed where roads cross so drivers will not crash their cars into each other.

story
(stories)
A **story** tells you about things that have happened. Some **stories** are real, while others are make-believe.

straw
A **straw** is a thin tube that you drink through. When you sip on a **straw**, you pull liquid into your mouth.

strawberry
(strawberries)
A **strawberry** is a small, soft red fruit with tiny seeds all over it. *Strawberry shortcake is a favorite summer dessert.*

street
A **street** is a road in a city or town that usually has buildings along each side.

string
1. **String** is a long, thin, ropelike material that people use to tie things together, such as packages. 2. Musical instruments, like a guitar, have wire **strings** that make sounds when your fingers tug at them.

such
1. **Such** means something has a particular quality. *The baby is **such** a happy little boy that he smiles all of the time.* 2. **Such** means like or similar to. *The girl wants something hot to drink, **such** as soup.*

sugar
Sugar is a grainy brown or white food that makes things sweet. Soda, candy, and icing have **sugar** in them.

summer
Summer is the hottest season of the year. **Summer** comes between spring and fall. *Our family went to the beach last **summer**.*

sun
The **sun** is the big, bright, yellowish star you see in the sky during the day. The **sun** keeps us warm and gives us light.

A B C D E F G H I J K L M N O P Q R S T U V W X Y Z

sundae

A **sundae** is a dessert in a dish with ice cream and tasty things sprinkled on the top. Ice cream **sundaes** can come with fruit, nuts, whipped cream, and sauce.

Sunday

Sunday is the first day of the week. Some people go to church on **Sunday**, while others like to relax on this weekend day.

sunglasses

You wear **sunglasses** on your face during sunny days to protect your eyes. The lenses in **sunglasses** are made of dark or colored plastic or glass.

sunny

(sunnier, sunniest)

It is **sunny** outside when the sun is shining brightly. *Our family likes to go to the beach on a **sunny** day.*

sure

If you are **sure** about something, you know that you are right. *I am **sure** the sun will set at six o'clock today.*

surprise

A **surprise** is something you did not know was going to happen.

sweater

A **sweater** is something you wear on the top part of your body and arms to keep you very warm. Some **sweaters** have buttons, while other sweaters pull over your head.

sweet

(sweeter, sweetest)

1. If a food or drink is **sweet**, it tastes like sugar. Candy is **sweet**. 2. If you say someone is very **sweet**, you think she is being kind. *You are very **sweet** to push the little girl on the swing.*

swim

(swims, swam, swimming)

When you **swim**, you use your arms and legs to move yourself through the water.

swing

(swings, swung, swinging)

1. When something **swings**, it moves back and forth in the air. *The weight on the tall grandfather clock **swings** as it goes* tick-tock. 2. A **swing** is a seat on the playground that hangs on two chains and moves back and forth when you move your legs.

T

taco

You make a **taco** by folding a thin tortilla around a spicy mixture of meat and cheese topped with vegetables. The tortilla for the **taco** can be made with flour or corn. The **taco** tortilla can be soft or crunchy. You eat a **taco** with your hands.

tail

A **tail** grows out of the back end of some animals' bodies. Animals use their **tails** for moving, showing feelings, and holding things. *The dog wagged its **tail** to say hello.*

talk

(talks, talked, talking)
When you **talk**, you say something. *The girl **talked** to her friend on the telephone.*

tall

(taller, tallest)
If someone or something is **tall**, it is very high above the ground. *The basketball player was so **tall** he could touch the basket.*

tape

A **tape** is a long strip of plastic, cloth, or paper with a sticky material on one side. You use **tape** to hold things together or hang a poster on the wall.

tea

Tea is a drink you make by pouring hot water over special dried leaves. You can add sugar, lemon, or milk to **tea**, which can be served hot or cold.

teach

(teaches, taught, teaching)
When you **teach** someone, you help that person learn new things. *My big brother is **teaching** me how to hold a baseball bat.*

teacher

A **teacher** is a person whose job is to help others learn things. Most **teachers** work in schools.

teddy bear

A **teddy bear** is a soft, cuddly toy that looks like a bear. Many children like to take their **teddy bears** to bed with them.

A B C D E F G H I J K L M N O P Q R S T U V W X Y Z

telephone

A **telephone** is a machine for talking to and listening to people who are far away. A **telephone** rings to let you know someone is calling you.

television

A **television** is a machine that picks up air waves and turns them into pictures and sounds. You might watch the news, cartoons, or a movie on **television**. TV is the short name for **television**.

ten

Ten is a number that is one more than nine. 9+1=10. *You have **ten** toes on your feet.*

tennis

In the game of **tennis**, players try to hit a ball over a net with racquets. **Tennis** is played on a hard court where the ball will bounce.

thank

(thanks, thanked, thanking)
When you **thank** people, you tell them how happy you are with something they did. *The old lady **thanked** the girl for shoveling the snow from her path.*

Thanksgiving

Thanksgiving is a holiday that happens in the United States every year on the fourth Thursday in November. **Thanksgiving** reminds you to be glad for the good things in your life. Many families share a turkey dinner on **Thanksgiving**.

the

The means a specific one. ***The** girl wants to eat **the** plum.*

them

Them means two or more people or things. *The three boxes belong to **them**.*

there

There means in, at, or to that place. *Please go over **there** by the chair, and wait for me.*

they

They is a word you use when you are talking about more than one person or thing. ***They** are going to share the large pizza for dinner.*

think

(thinks, thought, thinking)
1. When you **think** about something, you use your mind. *The girl is **thinking** of an answer to the question.* 2. **Think** can also mean to believe something is true. *I **think** I know how to fix the car.*

third

Third means the next one after the second one. *My friend in the yellow hat is the **third** one in line for the donuts.*

thirteen

Thirteen is a number that is one more than twelve. 12+1=13. Some people think **thirteen** is an unlucky number.

thirty

Thirty is a number that means three groups of ten. 10+10+10=30.

this

This means one that is close or near by. ***This*** *blanket is keeping me warm.*

thousand

A **thousand** is a number that is ten times one hundred. 10x100=1,000.

three

Three is a number that stands for one more than two. 2+1=3. *People eat **three** meals a day.*

thumb

Your **thumb** is the shortest of your five fingers. You pick up things between your **thumb** and fingers.

thumb

Thursday

Thursday is the fifth day of the week. **Thursday** comes after Wednesday.

tiger

A **tiger** is a jungle animal that looks like a big cat with orange fur and black stripes.

time

1. **Time** is how long something takes to happen. **Time** is measured in seconds, minutes, hours, days, weeks, months, and years. 2. **Time** is the hours and minutes shown on a clock. *The **time** is three o'clock.*

tire

A **tire** is a circle of rubber that fits over a wheel and is usually filled with air. Cars and bikes ride on **tires**.

toad

A **toad** is a small brown-and-green animal that looks like a frog with thick, bumpy skin. A **toad** uses two large back legs to hop on land.

toast

Toast is a kind of brown, crispy bread cooked in a toaster. People make **toast** by heating it, and then they sometimes put butter and jam on it.

toaster

A **toaster** is a small machine that cooks bread. Each opening in the top of the **toaster** holds one slice.

today

Today means at the present day or time. *Today I am going to go to the tennis match.*

toe

A **toe** is one of the five small parts that is at the end of your foot.

toe

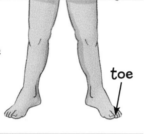

tomato

(tomatoes)

A **tomato** is a juicy, round, red fruit that grows on a vine. You can eat a **tomato** raw or cooked in a salad, sandwich, soup, or sauce.

tongue

Your **tongue** is the soft, moving, pink part inside your mouth. Your **tongue** helps you to taste things, swallow food, and speak.

tonight

Tonight is the night or the evening of this day. *We are going to hear a bedtime story tonight.*

tooth

(teeth)

A **tooth** is a hard, white thing in your mouth that you use for biting and chewing.

toothache

A **toothache** is a pain that you get in your tooth. If you eat too much sugary food, like candy, you might get a **toothache**.

toothbrush

(toothbrushes)

A **toothbrush** has a long handle with bristles on one end. You put toothpaste on a **toothbrush** to clean your teeth after you eat.

toothpaste

Toothpaste is a cleaner for your teeth that comes in tubes. You squeeze thick, creamy **toothpaste** onto your brush.

toward

Toward means to go in the direction of something. *The farmer quickly walked toward his cow.*

towel

A **towel** is a large, thick, soft cloth you use to dry yourself after taking a bath.

town

A **town** is a place with lots of streets, houses, buildings, and stores where many people live and work.

toy

A **toy** is something you play with to have fun. Dolls, balls, and games are **toys**.

toy box

(toy boxes)

A **toy box** is a container that holds toys, like balls, blocks, and stuffed animals. When you clean up toys, you can put them in the **toy box**.

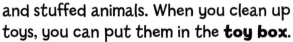

train

(trains, trained, training)

1. If you **train** your pet, you teach it how to do something. *I **trained** my dog to catch a stick.* 2. You can travel on tracks in a **train** pulled by an engine.

trash

Trash is something that is not any good, like junk or garbage, that people throw away. *The man threw his paper cup in the **trash**.*

trash can

A **trash can** is a large container made of metal or plastic with a lid. You throw garbage in a **trash can**.

travel

(travels, traveled, traveling)

When you **travel**, you go from one place to another. *I **traveled** to school on the yellow school bus.*

tree

A **tree** is a tall, woody plant with a trunk and branches. Some trees have leaves, while others have needles.

triangle

A **triangle** is a shape with three straight sides and three corners.

tricycle

A **tricycle** is a toy with three wheels and a seat that you ride. You pedal a **tricycle** and steer it with a handlebar.

trombone

A **trombone** is a long, curved, brass musical instrument that makes a sound when you blow into it. One end of the **trombone** slides in and out.

trophy
(trophies)

A **trophy** is a prize you get when you win a game or race. Sometimes a **trophy** has your name on it.

truck

A **truck** is a big vehicle with large wheels that carries things in the back. A driver rides in the front of a **truck**.

trumpet

A **trumpet** is a curved, brass instrument that makes a sound when you blow into it. You push three valves on the **trumpet** to change the sounds it makes.

try
(tries, tried, trying)

1. If you **try** something, you are testing it out. *I **tried** the salad to see if I liked it.*
2. When you **try** to do something, you attempt to do it. *I **try** to help my mom.*

T-shirt

A **T-shirt** is something with short-sleeves that covers the top of your body. Many **T-shirts** have words or pictures on them.

tuba

A **tuba** is a huge brass instrument that makes low sounds when you blow into it.

Tuesday

Tuesday is the third day of the week. **Tuesday** comes after Monday.

turkey

A **turkey** is a big bird that can raise its tail into a fan shape. **Turkeys** live on a farm or in the wild. People like to eat **turkey** at Thanksgiving.

turtle

A **turtle** is an animal with wrinkly skin and a hard shell. A **turtle** can hide inside its shell.

twelve

Twelve is a number that is one more than eleven. 11+1=12. **Twelve** is also sometimes called a dozen, such as a dozen eggs.

12

twenty

Twenty is a number that is two groups of ten. 10+10=20.

20

two

Two is the number that comes after one. 1+1=2. *You have **two** eyes.*

2

umbrella

An **umbrella** has a round cloth or plastic top and a long handle with a curved end. You hold an **umbrella** over your head to stay dry when it rains.

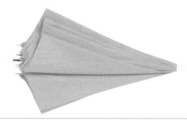

umpire

An **umpire** is a person who makes sure the players follow the rules in sports, such as baseball.

uncertain

If something is **uncertain**, it may change at any time. *It is **uncertain** if the rain will stay away for our picnic.*

uncle

Your **uncle** is the brother of your father or your mother, or the husband of your aunt.

under

If something is **under** something else, it is below it. *The pear is **under** the two lemons.*

understand

(understands, understood, understanding) If you **understand** something, you know what it means. *I **understand** the directions for building the toy race car.*

underwear

Underwear is clothing you wear under other clothes next to your skin. Underpants and undershirts are **underwear**.

A B C D E F G H I J K L M N O P Q R S T U V W X Y Z

unhappy
(unhappier, unhappiest)
If you are **unhappy**, you are sad or upset about something. *You are **unhappy** that your goldfish died.*

uniform
A **uniform** is a set of clothes that people wear to show they do a certain job or belong to a certain group. *Nurses, firefighters, athletes, and Brownies and Cub Scouts all wear **uniforms**.*

until
Until means up to the time something happens. *The girl waited to cross the street **until** the traffic light changed.*

unzip
(unzips, unzipped, unzipping)
When you **unzip** something, you move the zipper along a track and open it up. *The lady **unzips** her sweater.*

up
If somebody or something goes **up**, it moves from a lower level to a higher one. *The airplane goes **up** in the sky.*

Uranus
Uranus is a planet in the solar system. **Uranus** is the third largest planet and seventh planet from the Sun.

us
Us is another way to say we. *Please give the tennis balls to **us**.*

use
(uses, used, using)
When you **use** something, you are doing a job with it. *You **use** a hammer and nails to build a house.*

A B C D E F G H I J K L M N O P Q R S T U V W X Y Z

V

vacation

A **vacation** is a time off from work and school.
A **vacation** is often a time for fun and trips.

vacuum cleaner

A **vacuum cleaner** is a machine that sucks up dirt. You use a **vacuum cleaner** to clean rugs, floors, and curtains.

valentine

A **valentine** is a greeting card that you send to people you like on Valentine's Day. *Many valentines have **heart**-shape designs.*

Valentine's Day

Valentine's Day is a holiday that takes place on February 14. On **Valentine's Day** you send cards, flowers, or candy to people you love.

van

A **van** is a kind of vehicle. It is like a small bus. **Vans** usually have three or more seats. **Vans** are bigger than cars.

vase

A **vase** is a tall, thin container made out of glass that holds water. You can put fresh flowers in a **vase**.

vegetable

A **vegetable** is a plant that you eat for food. Carrots, peas, and broccoli are **vegetables**.

Venus

Venus is a planet in the solar system. **Venus** is the second planet from the Sun.

very

You use the word **very** before another word to make it show a greater amount. *The elephant is **very** big.*

vest

A **vest** is a sleeveless jacket worn on the top part of your body over a shirt. A **vest** can be part of a suit.

view

A **view** is what you see from a particular place. *The **view** of the flowers from the top of the hill is beautiful.*

vine

A **vine** is a plant with a long, winding stem that grows along the ground or up trees. *Squash grows on a **vine**.*

violet

A **violet** is a small sweet-smelling flower with five petals. **Violets** are purple, white, yellow, or pink.

violin

A **violin** is a wooden instrument that has four strings. You play the **violin** by moving a bow across the strings.

visit

(visits, visited, visiting)
When you **visit** someone or something, you go to see that person or thing. *The girls are **visiting** the library to get books.*

voice

Your **voice** is the sound you make when you talk or sing.

volleyball

A **volleyball** is a round, white ball about the size of a soccer ball. You hit a **volleyball** over a net during the game of **volleyball**.

vulture

A **vulture** is a large bird that does not have any feathers on its head. **Vultures** eat animals that are already dead.

W

waffle

A **waffle** is a crisp, bumpy cake cooked in a waffle iron. *We had **waffles** with butter and syrup for breakfast.*

wag

(wags, wagged, wagging)
To **wag** means to move back and forth. *The dog was **wagging** his tail.*

wagon

A **wagon** carries people and things from place to place. **Wagons** can be pulled by hand, by horses, or by a tractor.

wait

(waits, waited, waiting)
If you **wait**, you stay in one place until something happens. *We **waited** by the toaster for the toast to pop up.*

walk

(walks, walked, walking)
When you **walk**, you put one foot in front of the other and move along.

wall

1. A **wall** is one side of a room. 2. A **wall** is something you make with stones or bricks to separate one person's land from another's.

wallet

A **wallet** is a small folder for money that you carry in your pocket or purse.

walnut

A **walnut** is a thick, hard-shelled nut from a tree. You can eat the soft, chewy nut inside.

wand

A **wand** is a small, thin stick you hold in your hand. A magician waves a **wand** to perform magic tricks.

want

(wants, wanted, wanting)
If you **want** something, you would like to have it. *The girl **wants** some peanut butter for her sandwich.*

war

When armies or groups of people fight against each other, they are at **war**.

warm

(warmer, warmest)

If you are **warm**, you are fairly hot and no longer cold. *The boy wears his fuzzy hat to keep his head* ***warm.***

was

(be, am, are, is, were, been, being)

Was means something occurred. *She* ***was*** *playing volleyball this morning.*

wash

(washes, washed, washing)

To **wash** is to clean something with soap and water. You **wash** your hands before you eat.

washcloth

A **washcloth** is a small square cloth you use to wash your face and body with soap and water.

waste

(wastes, wasted, wasting)

If you **waste** something, you are using more of it than you need. *Do not* ***waste*** *all of the toothpaste on your brush.*

watch

(watches, watched, watching)

1. When you **watch** someone or something, you look at that person or thing to see what is happening. *You* ***watch*** *the bee fly to the flower.* 2. A **watch** is a small clock you wear on your wrist.

water

Water is a clear liquid without any smell or taste. **Water** falls from the sky in the form of rain. You can drink **water** or take a bath in it.

watermelon

A **watermelon** is a large, juicy fruit with a thick green skin. Inside, the **watermelon** is crisp and pink with many seeds.

wave

(waves, waved, waving)

1. You say hello or good-bye to someone when you **wave** your hand side to side. 2. A **wave** is a high, curved line of water moving across the ocean. *The boy rides the surfboard on the* ***waves.***

way

1. The **way** you do something is how you do it. *This is the **way** you make the bed.*
2. A **way** is how you get from one place to another. *This is the **way** from my house to town.*

we

When the speaker includes others, she says **we**. ***We** went for a hike to the pond.*

wear

(wears, wore, worn, wearing)
1. When you **wear** clothes, they cover your body. *I am **wearing** my snowsuit and hat to play outdoors in the cold.*
2. If something **wears** out, it has been used a lot of times and is no longer as good or as strong. *The car tires went flat when they **wore** out.*

weather

The **weather** is what it is like outdoors: sunny, windy, hot, cold, or rainy. *I am wearing a bathing suit for the hot **weather**.*

wedding

A **wedding** is a marriage ceremony and celebration when a man and a woman become husband and wife.

Wednesday

Wednesday is the fourth day of the week. **Wednesday** comes after Tuesday.

week

A **week** is seven days. There are 52 **weeks** in a year.

weigh

(weighs, weighed, weighing)
You put something on a scale and **weigh** it to see how heavy it is. *The potatoes **weighed** ten pounds.*

weird

(weirder, weirdest)
If something is **weird**, it looks or acts strange. *The monster looks **weird** with two heads.*

A B C D E F G H I J K L M N O P Q R S T U V W X Y Z

welcome

(welcomes, welcomed, welcoming) When you **welcome** people, you give them a pleasant greeting. *The girl **welcomes** her friend to the party.*

well

(better, best)

1. If you do something **well**, you do it in a good way. *The man and woman danced very **well** together.* 2. If you are feeling **well**, you are healthy and not sick.

were

(be, am, are, is, was, been, being)

Were is used to show that something occurred. *The children **were** running down the hill to the park.*

west

West is a direction. The sun sets in the **west** in the evening.

wet

(wetter, wettest)

When something is **wet**, it is full of water, like a **wet** sponge, or covered with water, like a **wet** road. *The friends got **wet** when they went swimming.*

whale

A **whale** is a huge ocean animal that looks like a fish but is really a mammal. *A blue **whale** breathes through a spout in its head and is the largest animal in the world.*

what

When you use **what,** you ask about the identity or makeup of something. *Do you know **what** questions the teacher will ask on the quiz?*

wheat

Farmers grow **wheat**, a type of grain on tall stalks. We grind the **wheat** seeds to make flour for bread.

wheel

A **wheel** is shaped like a circle and rolls around. A **wheel** moves things along the ground, like cars, bicycles, and skateboards.

wheelchair

A **wheelchair** is a type of seat with large wheels. You use a **wheelchair** when you are sick or cannot walk.

when

You use **when** to ask or tell about a particular time. *Do you know **when** the movie begins?*

where

You use **where** when you want to know about a place. ***Where** should I hang my coat?*

whether

You use **whether** when you want to know if it is or was true that something happened. *Do you know **whether** or not the train left on time?*

which

You use **which** when you want to know about a specific person or thing. ***Which** piece of fruit will the boy choose, the apple or the banana?*

while

While means at the same time as something else is happening. *The girl played a game on the computer **while** her friend read a book.*

whiskers

Whiskers are long, stiff hairs that grow on a man's face, like a beard. **Whiskers** also grow on either side of the nose on the faces of some animals, such as a cat.

whisper

(whispers, whispered, whispering)
When people **whisper**, they speak in a very quiet, low voice. *The girl **whispers** a secret in her friend's ear, so no one else can hear it.*

whistle

A **whistle** is a small instrument that, when someone blows into it, makes a sharp, high-pitched sound. Police officers blow **whistles** to move traffic along.

white

When something has no color, it is **white**. Snow is **white**.

who

When you use **who,** you are asking about the identity of a particular person or group. ***Who** do you think ate all of the Halloween candy?*

whole

If something is **whole**, it has all of its parts and is not broken. *The last cookie on the plate is **whole**.*

A B C D E F G H I J K L M N O P Q R S T U V W X Y Z

why

Why means for what reason, cause, or purpose. *The boy asks his teacher **why** the duck has webbed feet.*

wide

The distance from one side of something to the other is how **wide** it is. *A car is too **wide** to go on that patch.*

wife

(wives)

A man's **wife** is the woman he married.

will

Will refers to something that is going to happen in the future. *Debbie **will** carry the groceries for her grandmother.*

win

(wins, won, winning)

When you come in first in a race or a game or do better than other players, you **win**. *The boy **won** first prize in the chess match.*

wind

Wind is fast-moving air. *The **wind** blows the leaves down the street.*

window

A **window** is an opening in a hall or car that lets in sunlight and air. Most **windows** are covered in glass.

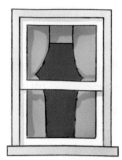

wing

A **wing** is a part of a bird's body that helps it to fly. Birds, bats, and insects flap their **wings** to fly. A metal airplane **wing** does not flap.

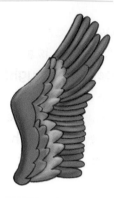

winter

Winter is the season that comes between fall and spring. **Winter** is the coldest season of the year.

wipe

(wipes, wiped, wiping)

If you **wipe** something, you clean or dry it by rubbing it with a cloth. *The boy **wiped** the dishes with a towel.*

wise

(wiser, wisest)

If someone is very **wise**, she is aware of what is going on, and she has good sense. *The **wise** girl brought along an umbrella in case of rain.*

wish
(wishes, wished, wishing)
If you **wish** for something, you want it or hope very much that it will happen. *The boy* **wishes** *for a puppy for his birthday.*

witch
(witches)
A **witch** is a person thought to have magic power. In stories, **witches** might ride on brooms or cast spells.

with
1. If you are doing something **with** someone, you are doing it together. *The boy is playing* **with** *his friend.* 2. You may use **with** to show that someone is using something. *The lady is writing* **with** *a pen.*

without
Without means something is missing. *The girl had to play the piano* **without** *her sheet music.*

wolf
(wolves)
A **wolf** is a wild animal that looks like a dog with a pointed nose, pointed ears, and sharp teeth.

woman
(women)
A **woman** is a grown-up girl.

wonderful
If something is **wonderful,** it is excellent. *My new haircut is* **wonderful.**

wood
Wood is the hard part of the tree that comes from the trunk and branches. You can build houses and furniture with **wood**.

woodpecker
A **woodpecker** is a bird that taps holes in trees with its long, sharp beak. A **woodpecker** finds insects to eat in the small holes and makes a nest in the large trees.

word
A **word** is a group of sounds and letters that means something when put together. When you speak or write, you use **words**.

A B C D E F G H I J K L M N O P Q R S T U V W X Y Z

work
(works, worked, working)
1. **Work** is when you do a job or something that needs to be done. *My mommy **works** as a doctor.* 2. When something **works**, it runs smoothly and does what it is supposed to do. *My flashlight **works** with the new batteries.*

world
The **world** is the planet we live on, with all of the people and the things in it.

worm
A **worm** is a long, thin animal without arms and legs that lives in dirt. **Worms** are soft and small.

worry
(worries, worried, worrying)
If you **worry,** you feel anxious that something bad might happen. *I **worry** that my scary nightmares will come true.*

worse
(bad, worst)
If something is getting **worse**, it means it is already bad and getting very bad. *My hurt finger is much **worse** today.*

would
Would means to have a wish or desire to do something. *I **would** like to have one dollar to buy ice cream.*

wreath
A **wreath** is a pretty wall hanging. **Wreaths** are often made from small branches or straw. You decorate a **wreath** with flowers, ribbons, and ornaments.

write
(writes, wrote, written, writing)
To **write** is to mark letters and numbers with a pen or pencil on a surface. People most often write on paper.

writer
A **writer** is a person who puts her thoughts down on paper or at the computer and writes for a job. A **writer** writes books and articles for magazines and newspapers.

wrong
Wrong means something is not right. *We took the **wrong** turn in the road, and now we are lost.*

X

X-ray

An **X-ray** is a photograph of your insides. You can see your bones on an **X-ray**.

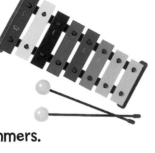

xylophone

A **xylophone** is a musical instrument with rows of wooden or metal bars. You play a **xylophone** by hitting the bars with small hammers.

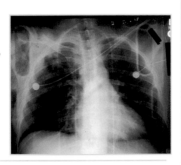

yard

1. A **yard** is a measurement. There are three feet in one **yard** on a yardstick.
2. A **yard** is an open area next to a building with flowers or bushes. *The children like to play in the **yard**.*

yawn

(yawns, yawned, yawning)
When you **yawn**, you open your mouth wide and breathe in and out because you are tired. Sometimes people stretch their arms out when they **yawn**.

year

A **year** is a measure of time. There are twelve months in one **year**.

yell

(yells, yelled, yelling)
When you **yell**, you open your mouth and shout loudly.

yellow

Yellow is a bright, sunny color. Lemons, bananas, and egg yolks are **yellow** foods.

yes

You use **yes** to show you agree. *Yes, I will help you clean up the yard.*

yet

Yet means up to this time. *The baby cannot feed herself **yet**.*

you

You means the person being addressed. *You must meet me at the store.*

young
(younger, youngest)
A person or an animal that is **young** has lived only for a short time. *A colt is a **young** horse that still needs its mother.*

your
Your means that it relates or belongs to you. *This is **your** big brass tuba.*

yo-yo
A **yo-yo** is a round toy that looks like a flat spool on a string. The string winds around the **yo-yo** so you can make it go up and down and spin.

zero
Zero is another name for nothing. A **zero** is a math symbol that means none.

zip
(zips, zipped, zipping)
If you **zip** something, you open and close it with a zipper. ***Zip** up your sweater so you will stay warm.*

zipper
A **zipper** is a clothes fastener with two rows of metal or plastic teeth. You can have a **zipper** on your jeans or jacket.

zoo
A **zoo** is a place where wild animals, such as tigers and elephants, are kept so that people can come and see them.

zucchini
(zucchini)
Zucchini is a squash that is dark green on the outside and white on the inside. **Zucchini** grows on vines.

zebra
A **zebra** is an African animal that looks like a striped horse.